12-31-59

THE NEGRO PRESS RE-EXAMINED

THE NEGRO PRESS
RE-EXAMINED

Political Content of Leading Negro Newspapers

BY

MAXWELL R. BROOKS, Ph.D.

THE CHRISTOPHER PUBLISHING HOUSE
BOSTON, U.S.A.

1101927

THIS

VOLUME IS DEDICATED

TO

Mary Emily Brooks

ACKNOWLEDGEMENTS

The preparation of this manuscript in its present form would never have been accomplished had it not been for the helpful criticism of Professors Brewton Berry and Raymond Sletto. The more fatiguing moments have been lightened by their encouragement. Other persons too numerous to mention have contributed materially to whatever merit this study may have. The late Robert E. Park, and Frederick G. Detweiler, both students of the sociology of journalism, gave counsel some years ago that has been invaluable in this project. The writer wishes also to acknowledge his indebtedness to the gentlemen of the Associated Negro Press, and to the many publishers and editors who have made their files available, and have in many other ways been helpful. The writer alone is responsible for any errors that may be found in these pages.

CONTENTS

9

INTRODUCTION

The history of the American Negro is an epic without equal or parallel. No other racial or ethnic group can point to so varied and harrowing a series of experiences crowded into the brief span of three or four centuries. Torn from his native habitat, forcibly transported across the ocean, subjected to the humiliations of slavery, stripped of his ancestral culture, he finally won emancipation through a bitter, fratricidal war.

For nearly a hundred years now the Negro's efforts have been directed toward the achievement of full citizenship. While other minorities may resist assimilation, and others regard it with bewilderment or ambivalence, the Negro has persistently striven for the privilege of participating fully in the life of the society of which he has so long been an integral part.

This long struggle for status has not been one of steady, uphill progress. The obstacles along the path have been numerous, formidable, and ingenious. There have been long periods of reversals and frustrations capable of trying the faith and patience of all but the most persistent. It is only within the past few decades that the victories have been sufficiently numerous and significant to suggest that the goal of equality may be attainable after all.

Two institutions have had major roles in this long struggle — the church and the press. White Americans are rather well aware of the part that the Negro church and its agents have played, but they are far less informed about the Negro press.

11

The Negro press had its beginning early in the nineteenth century, and throughout its long existence it has been a powerful instrument in molding Negro opinion behind the crusade for full citizenship. The dissemination of news has always been one of its functions, and this is becoming increasingly true nowadays. However, it has performed a variety of functions, and certainly protest has been one of its most characteristic and effective.

It is not surprising, accordingly, that the Negro press has been the object of much criticism. It has been charged with being excessively sensational, superficial, bawdy, and imitative. It has also, from time to time, been accused of being communistic, radical, un-American, and inflammatory. Howbeit, the Negro press has been important, which none will deny, and it deserves more thorough study than it has received.

Dr. Brooks, in this monograph, has made a careful, scholarly inquiry into the content of the Negro press. His approach has been objective, and his method of analysis as scientific as possible. He has made a valuable contribution to our understanding and evaluation of a most important American institution.

BREWTON BERRY
Professor of Sociology and Anthropology
The Ohio State University

The Negro Press Re-examined

CHAPTER I

THE PROBLEM

A. INTRODUCTION

During the last quarter century the Negro news-paper in America has made significant progress, both as an economic institution, and as a cultural influence in the lives of the Negro people. Between the two world wars this minority press began to take on a pro-fessional character. Evidence of this maturity is to be found in the growing number of trained journalists and career writers who are exerting a positive influence on the quality of the content of these journals. There has also been a marked increase in circulation. Total circulation has approximately doubled during this period. The expansion in the capital investment in plants and equipment has been equally significant.

It may prove helpful if we classify the Negro week-lies into the three following categories. There are the nationally known papers with circulations that run into six figures. These journals are published in two or more editions — city and national, state and/or regional editions. This development makes an appeal to the interests of reading publics in various sections of the nation and has apparently aided in extending the cir-culation of these newspapers. They are incorporated business enterprises, the valuation placed on a few such plants being well over a quarter-million dollars each. In addition to the press services, they maintain their own staff writers and correspondents. These newspapers may be purchased on news stands throughout the nation. A second group of the Negro papers with circulations ranging from 10,000 to 50,000, is numerically much larger than the first. There are about twenty papers in this category and not more than a half dozen in the former bracket. Many of the latter papers, however, like those in the former group, are well established enterprises, some having been founded more than a half century ago. They are published in the large cities in every geographical region except the northwest. Unlike the first group of papers, however, they are not so well known, or as widely circulated.

The third category includes the vast majority of the Negro newspapers. Few publications in this latter group are audited. They are minor sheets and are published chiefly in the smaller cities, although a few occupy a marginal status in the big urban centers. A considerable amount of instability is to be found among the papers in this bracket. New ventures in publication are begun from time to time and soon disappear, while others face a hazardous and uncertain future.

The day of the undisciplined enthusiast has about passed. In the modern group of working journalists are to be found experienced and nationally known writers and authors. Their journalistic and literary productions are not confined to the Negro press, but also appear in well known national magazines, and are published by many of the nations' leading publishing houses.

The Negro newspapers came into existence before the Civil War as a medium of expression of abolitionist sentiment, and played an important part in that crusade. They have never ceased to be critical of the American social order. While at the close of the Civil War the Negro achieved a nominal citizenship status, the freedom and equality guaranteed him under the law have never been fully realized. Much of the literary productivity of the Negro has likewise been concerned with this problem.

Lately the Negro papers have been the subject of considerable criticism themselves, this criticism growing out of their outspoken demands for civil liberties for the Negro people, and their denunciation of many practices in American life held by them to be undemocratic. Other critical comment directed at these newspapers has been concerned with an appraisal of their professional quality. More specifically, some critics have alleged that they are unduly sensational in their news emphasis. It has also been asserted that their advertising policies are questionable. The supplemental character of these newspapers, or "race angling", as it is sometimes called, has been the subject of criticism by some. It is not always clear, however, why this emphasis should be regarded as grounds for criticism. This study will devote some attention to a consideration of these issues.

Some students have tended to characterize the role of the Negro press today as being primarily that of Negro protest.[1] The news function is considered by them to be of secondary importance. Since this viewpoint seems to have become rather widely, and perhaps uncritically accepted, the writer set himself the task

---

[1] Burma, John H. "An Analysis of the Present Negro Press," *Social Forces*, XXVI, No. 2 (1947), pp. 172-180; Davie, M.R. *Negroes in American Society.* New York: McGraw Hill Co., 1949, p. 197.

of submitting this theory to a quantitative examination. This research interest may be considered in the nature of a secondary hypothesis; secondary, that is, to the main concern of this investigation, the alleged subversive character of the Negro newspapers.

It has been more than hinted by various persons of some standing, that some of the leading Negro journals were "leftist", or "communist inspired". This has been denied by others. This study grew out of an urge, on the part of this student, to find an answer to this question that would be verifiable and free of bias. The answer that is given in this study rests upon an analysis of the political content of the leading Negro newspapers. It was the implications of their political views that constituted the focal point of popular controversy. While an examination of the history of the Negro press in America is a necessary precondition to an understanding of the problem, or problems, being considered here, the basic methodology employed in this research, however, is quantitative (see Chapter II, Methodology). It is held by the investigator that in this problem area there is considerable room for subjectivity and bias, and that an objective, controlled study would minimize the personal factor.

B. CRITICISM OF THE NEGRO PRESS

During the recent war period, political attitudes expressed in the publications of racial and national minorities became a matter of national concern. It was during this time that the content of Negro newspapers attracted considerable attention, and some of them became the subject of heated controversy. Even prior to the entry of the United States into the war this country had assumed the self-styled role of the "arsenal of democracy". From that time on, the nation found itself engaged in a war in which racial and political ideologies played a more prominent role than ever before in history. Curiously enough, some of "the democracies" — the declared enemies of German racism — had long historical records of racial discrimination and segregation unparalleled even by the Germans. And, while the Negro newspapermen had no illusions about the place of racial minorities in a Fascist dominated world, they were far from giving an unqualified vote of confidence to the Western Allies, particularly to the United States.

The Press and the War. Mental reservations associated with all-out support of America's war effort were evident in the editorial opinion of many Negro newspapers consulted by this investigator. The following quotations were taken from editions of these newspapers immediately following the attack on Pearl Harbor. They represent newspapers of all sizes, and are geographically distributed from New York City to the west coast. All of the five leading newspapers with the national circulations, on which this study is primarily based, are represented in this group. The opinions expressed were as follows:

> The *Pittsburgh Courier* solemnly pledges its "all-out" effort to keep the banner of liberty, justice, and equality flying over our ramparts. The *Pittsburgh Courier, however** also pledges to continue unrelenting warfare against the enemies within our gates. (Dec. 13, 1941)

Said the *Chicago Defender:*

> War is upon us . . . we must stand united against this common enemy and beat him away from our shores. *But** we have some internal problems of our own to settle before we can present a solid united front. (Dec. 13, 1941)

* Italics, the writer's

From the *Cleveland Herald* we get this comment:

As in all wars, the Negro in these United States is ready to answer his country's call. *Despite** . . . the denial of opportunity and equality. (Dec. 13, 1941)

The *St. Louis Argus:* Of course, we as Negroes, and as American citizens, are ready and willing to do our bit in the defense of this country in times of National peril, *but** it is galling to our sense of right and justice when we are denied the rights and privileges to serve our country in any branch of the armed forces, just as other Americans do. (Dec. 13, 1941)

The *Oklahoma Eagle:* So as America goes to war, let us feel that this is OUR WAR . . . Let us fight against the injustices of Southern tradition *but** let us give everything that we have, not necessarily for the preservation of the American way of life, but for what America stands. (Dec. 13, 1941)

The *Gary American:* The American Negro re-pledges his allegiance to his flag, and to his country . . . we do it *not unmindful of** the mistreatment to which we are now subjected. (Dec. 12, 1941)

The *Amsterdam News:* We must win this war . . . *But** to win we will need our all. This is no time for superficial distinctions, based upon skin color. This is no time for subversive race prejudice. (Dec. 13, 1941)

The *Louisiana Weekly:* In this hour of national crisis, Negroes pledge full support to the President and the government. *More than that,** they demand the opportunity to share equally the defense of the Nation. (Dec. 20, 1941)

The *Black Dispatch:* Every American Negro should help the navy, the army and air corps, and all units of our military establishments, *and** every American Negro should while shouldering his full responsibility of citizenship continue to demand every right of citizenship. (Dec. 13, 1941)

The *Detroit Tribune:* We must win the war. As colored Americans, we do not enjoy all the freedoms we should, *but** the freedom we have is worth fighting for. (Dec. 20, 1941)

The *Louisville Ledger:* The Negro American will do his part . . . *But** this is not all— White Americans must at once extend

---

* Italics, the writer's

to us the hand of full fellowship in order that the greatest good may be forthcoming. It is entirely up to them. Will they do it? (Dec. 13, 1941)

The *Afro-American:* Now with the enemy at our door, we say again to our fellow Americans . . . *Take down the color bar** . . . We cannot defend America with a dust brush, a mop and a white apron. We cannot march against enemy planes and tanks, and challenge warships armed only with a whiskbroom and a wide grin. (Dec. 20, 1941)

The *California Eagle:* When the United States is threatened hourly with bomb attack . . . *The continued practice of segregating** one-tenth of the American population . . . can only breed bitterness and disunity. (Dec. 18, 1941)

It would seem that the newspapers quoted here were less than enthusiastic about their pledged support of the war effort. There were, however, some responses that were less demanding of America, and less critical. For example The *St. Louis Call* says only;

There can be but one attitude toward this war among Negro Americans. That attitude must be the same as other Americans. (Dec. 12, 1941)

From the *St. Louis American:* Every citizen of the United States has but one course, one cause, one allegiance, and that to defend and sustain the country. (Dec. 11, 1941)

Among the five big nationally circulated papers, the *Journal and Guide,* of Norfolk, Virginia, was the only one to pledge all, and ask nothing in return. That journal's comment was as follows:

Always in every crisis through which the nation has passed, our people have contributed their lives and their labor without stint or limit. We crave the opportunity to serve . . . wherever we are called upon to go. (Dec. 13, 1941)

When the Japanese struck at Pearl Harbor on December 7, 1941, General George C. Marshall, the Army

---

* Italics, the writer's

Chief of Staff, had previously scheduled a press conference with Negro newspaper publishers for the morning of December 8. Although the impact of this sudden attack must have made exacting demands on the time of a Chief of Staff, yet General Marshall considered this engagement significant enough to keep. Whatever he may have said concerning the existing policy of segregation in the armed forces, a subject of attack by the press, or on the problem of morale in general, it failed to placate these newspapermen. The excerpts previously quoted from various editorials were published after this meeting.

Quite apparently the United States was caught in a moral dilemma, for, while allegedly fighting German racism abroad, this country maintained a policy of racial segregation at home. The South, so it was alleged, preferred losing the war to giving up its segregation. The Negro newspapers never eased up their pressure on this critical issue as the war progressed. The *Pittsburgh Courier* popularized the double V slogan, "Victory at home and abroad"; while, according to the *Amsterdam News*, "V can also stand for Vassal, as well as for Victory".

The editorial that follows is representative of much that was to be found in most Negro newspapers at the time:

> Those who have any knowledge concerning the plight of the Negro in America are naturally skeptical of the position the Negro may assume in this present conflict. Negroes returned from the battle fields of France to lynch mobs in the South and unemployment in the North . . . they were discouraged and disgusted with the conditions under which they were forced to live throughout the country.
>
> Negroes (now) are deeply conscious of the discrimination and segregation accorded them by both branches of the Government's armed forces: the army and navy; that there is a general denial of civil and political rights throughout a large section of the

country; that discrimination in the National Defense program is all too common; that there is discrimination in many branches of the government itself; that foreigners — often unable to speak the English language — are given the very opportunities denied deserving and loyal Negro citizens; that the government itself has exhibited an unwillingness to remedy these faults. Because of these shortcomings, and millions of others, much concern is felt regarding the attitude of the Negro . . . *Louisiana Weekly* (Dec. 20, 1941)

The Negro newspapers were not entirely alone in their criticism of American racial policies. Many liberal white publications, and some not so liberal, gave attention to this problem. *Harper's Magazine* carried a critical review of the conduct of the war, "American Negroes and the War", by Earl Brown, former editor of the *Amsterdam News.*[2] The newspaper *P.M.* featured a series of articles on April 7-10, 1942, entitled "What Are We Fighting For?" Three of the four contributors were Negroes, including Roy Wilkins, editor of the *Crisis,* a Negro magazine. The fourth article was written by the late Wendell Willkie. The *Saturday Evening Post*[3] published an article, "It's Our Country Too", written by the late Walter White, who had a column in the *Chicago Defender.* Also, the *New Republic,*[4] *Survey Graphic*[5] and other journals, did special numbers on the color problem, all of which enabled the minority viewpoint to reach a wider audience.

The Birmingham, Alabama *News,* a white daily, editorialized:

Here in America we have a problem of our own which should be faced frankly. In this country are 10,000,000 Negroes. They are being called upon to fight, to risk and to sacrifice, just as all

---

[2] *Harper's* Magazine, April, 1942.
[3] December 14, 1940.
[4] October 18, 1943.
[5] November, 1942.

the other inhabitants of this country. They are doing that will-
ingly. There has just been graduated at Tuskegee Institute the
Nation's first class of Negro flying cadets. One of Alabama's
first casualties at Pearl Harbor was a Negro.

But Negroes also want to be of service on the home front.
They want to be used in home defense activities. They want
a fair distribution of jobs growing out of the war as well as of
the danger at the front. They want to feel that the ideals for
which they are fighting mean something to them too.

These pleas by Negro leaders are not to go unanswered by the
white people of the nation if the country is to deserve the highest
loyalty and the best service from all citizens.[6]

Howard Vincent O'Brian, wrote in his column in the *Chicago Daily News*, March 5, 1942:

It seems to me that we should stop trying to peddle this war
as if it were nail polish or a cure for acid stomach. The quicker
we face up to it — and the part we play in it — the quicker we
will get on to something better. If we believe in democracy as
we say we do, then let us quickly set about the practice thereof.
And let us free ourselves from the delusion that other races will
believe in our promises of liberation when we are so skeptical of
liberty at home.

We promised freedom to the Negro. We never gave it. In
some parts of the nation the Negro cannot vote. In no part of
the nation does he have a chance to make a living on equal
terms with the white man.

The best goodwill mission we could send out to the world is
the news that we are practicing equality as well as preaching it.
And there isn't much time left.

Herbert Agar, editor of the *Louisville Courier Journal*, stated in rather blunt terms:

Either America must believe in and fight for the high principle
of all men to be free and participate in a democracy, or she must
renounce her ideals and admit Hitler is right.[7]

---

[6] An editorial from the Birmingham *News*, reprinted in the *Norfolk
Journal and Guide* April 4, 1942.

[7] Quoted from speech delivered in Houston, Texas. *Afro-American*,
June 23, 1941.

The question of Loyalty. It was this kind of expression, found alike in Negro and some white journals, that attracted the attention of another section of the white press. Virginius Dabney, a Southern gentleman, author, and editor of the Richmond, Virginia, *Times Dispatch,* was very much disturbed. In an article appearing in the *Atlantic Monthly,*[8] entitled "Nearer and Nearer the Precipice", he warned:

> A small group of Negro agitators and another small group of white rabble rousers are pushing the country closer and closer to an interracial explosion . . . the radical element of the Negro press, both North and South is stirring up interracial hate.

He charged further that these leaders are trying to force "the abolition of racial segregation throughout the United States, absolute enforcement of the Fifth, Fourteenth, and Fifteenth Amendments, and elimination of the poll tax." But, he said that "the South cannot be high pressured into submission on this issue."

He did admit, however, that it would be unfair "to intimate that the whole colored press is incendiary in its present attitude." He spoke highly of the *Norfolk Journal and Guide,* "one of the sanest and best edited colored newspapers in the United States." He spoke well of P.B. Young, its publisher, and Gordon B. Hancock, one of its columnists. But the *Pittsburgh Courier* was considered by Mr. Dabney to be "one of the most radical of the Negro newspapers." And he expressed the opinion that "If this sort of thing keeps up, it can have but one result. The white leaders in the South who have been responsible for much of the steady progress of the Negro in the past, and who can bring

---

[8] January, 1943. (Vol. 171, No. 1) pp. 94-100.

about a great deal more such progress in the future, will be driven into the opposition camp."

Mr. Dabney closed with the hope that "the disturbing elements on both sides of the color line can be muzzled for the duration . . . and we shall be able to get on with the war."

Westbrook Pegler, the Scripps-Howard newspaper columnist, likewise turned critic of the Negro newspapers. During the early stages of the second World War, he devoted his syndicated column to a denunciation of the Negro press.[9] Citing the *Chicago Defender* and the *Pittsburgh Courier* for special comment, he stated:

> Both are exploiting the war emergency as an opportunity to push the aspirations of the colored people and they are standard reading among colored men in the armed forces . . . (and)
> These Negro papers agitate violently and, I think, to the same dangerous degree that was alleged against Charles E. Coughlin's weekly.[10]

Mr. Pegler further alleged, "In neither paper is there any writing of the slightest distinction. . . . The written or editorial matter is of lower mediocrity at best."

"They (the Negro papers) are reminiscent," he said, "of Hearst at his worst in their sensationalism, and in their obvious, inflammatory bias in the treatment of news they resemble such one-sided publications as the *Communist Daily Worker* and Coughlin's *Social Justice*."

"Some of the advertisements," he asserted, "constitute a sordid exploitation for revenue only," being characterized by "Luck's genuine magnetic loadstones at a dollar a pair, one to attract, one to repel; Zodiacal

---

[9] April 28, 1942; also May 11, 1942.
[10] Coughlin's *Social Justice* had been banned as subversive.

incense to invite good luck, and a book, at $2.00, which, it is intimated, will impart to the reader power to be victorious in all undertakings."[11]

Aside from his adverse comment on advertising, Pegler's other points of criticism were not well taken. Roy Wilkins, an *Amsterdam News* columnist at the time, and now Secretary of the National Association for the Advancement of Colored People, commented:

> All the rest of the column was typical Pegler stuff, topped with a vicious opinion that the *Pittsburgh Courier* and the *Chicago Defender* are in the same category as Father Coughlin's *Social Justice.*
>
> Pegler's charge that Negro papers are subversive because they carry news of, and editorial protests against, the mistreatment of Negro citizens is absurd, but dangerous . . . .
>
> The Negro press need not worry about Pegler's opinion of its editorial matter. The better and larger Negro papers are well-written. Some of their columnists write better than Pegler . . .[12]

This latter view expressed by Wilkins, is shared by George Schuyler,[13] another well known Negro columnist. Schuyler says,

> "Editorial for editorial and column for column we are not afraid to place any of a dozen Negro newspapers along side the leading white newspapers . . ."

With regard to Pegler's charge that the Negro papers "agitate violently," Schuyler has this to say:

---

[11] The writer measured the column inches of advertising of all kinds in the city edition of the *Pittsburgh Courier* (April 11, 1942), then in his possession, which may help gain some perspective. There were 1327 column inches of advertising, of which 257½ inches were devoted to cosmetics of all kinds. Fifteen column inches were devoted to good luck charms, etc. Philip Morris Cigarettes had 42 column inches of advertising; The Pittsburgh Milk Company 50; The Streamline Food Markets 60; Octagon Soap 36; a popular brand of whiskey 29, to mention a few.

[12] *Amsterdam (Star) News,* May 9, 1942.

[13] The *Pittsburgh Courier,* May 9, 1942.

"If the Negro newspapers had remained mum about color discrimination and racial segregation in the Government and industry, and concerned themselves only with urging a war against fascism abroad, no one would be concerned with their writings, their advertisements or their gossip columns except Negroes. But they have challenged America's least reputable but most persistent 'way of life,' so Pegler and his ilk want them suppressed."

A Critique of Function. Al White, a white Washington correspondent for the Associated Press, expressed a view similar to that of Schuyler, when he suggested that "Negro newspapers have a mission to perform, and that they are attracting the attention of topnotch columnists is a sure sign they are accomplishing part of that mission."[14]

Robert G. Spivak, another white newspaperman, said of Pegler:

When he writes of Negroes, he does so in a vein that is derisive, contemptuous and full of disdain. He evidently regards Negroes as a people apart from the great bulk of citizenry.[15]

Marjorie McKenzie, a columnist for the *Pittsburgh Courier* feels somewhat the same, when she says, "What Mr. Pegler has tried to do is minimize the importance of the Negro press by making it seem to be inferior and ridiculous."[16]

Lee Casey, white editor of the Denver *Rocky Mountain News,* disagrees with Mr. Pegler on the function, as well as the quality of writing in the Negro papers. He says in part:

I read the *Chicago Defender* occasionally, and the *Pittsburgh Courier* almost every week. I also see the *Colorado Statesman* and *Denver Sun.*

It strikes me that, considering the job they have to do and

[14] Quoted in *Amsterdam News,* May 9, 1942.
[15] Ibid.
[16] The *Pittsburgh Courier,* May 9, 1942.

what they have to do it with, the performance of these publications is highly creditable.

They appeal to a minority group, to be sure. But that is true of many other publications, including newspapers and magazines designed for circulation among special groups. All minority publications necessarily select and even emphasize the items of special interest to their special readers. The so-called Negro press is no exception . . . it is the particular function and duty of the Negro press to remind Negroes of the honor and dignity of their traditions and of the achievements of men and women of their group, present as well as past.

Mr. Pegler calls that "race-angling" the news. Maybe that's the right term. In any case, the Negro press has a job to do and is trying to do it. It makes a special appeal, but that is its objective.

As for the merits or demerits of the Negro writers whose work Mr. Pegler regards as "of lower mediocrity," that is a matter of taste. I have heard of people who said similar things, or worse, about Mr. Pegler himself.

As for me, I find the Negro writers well up to standard. They have not had the opportunities that would have been open had their complexion been of a different shade, but they have done mighty well in spite of that. The columns of J.A. Rogers and A.N. Fields of the *Pittsburgh Courier* and Earl W. Mann of the *Colorado Statesman* for example, are scholarly, considered, temperate, well-constructed. I wish I could say the same thing of the output of some paler columnists I know.

Even if this were not so, it seems to me the men and women who produce the Negro press of America deserve commendation instead of castigation.[17]

Another critique of the Negro press, "A Negro looks at the Negro Press," that had wide popular circulation during the recent war period, was contributed by Dr. Warren H. Brown, a Negro, "born in the South and raised in the mid-west," as he puts it. The article was published under the auspices of the Council of Democracy where Dr. Brown was employed as Director of Negro Relations. It was carried by both the *Saturday*

---

[17] Reprinted in *Chicago Defender*, May 16, 1942.

Review of Literature[18] and the *Readers Digest*.[19] Significantly, however, the title was changed in the latter journal to read "A Negro Warns the Negro Press," and it was on the stands before the *Saturday Review* carrying the original article was available. In Dr. Brown's thinking the problem may be analyzed in simple terms. He says:

> My race in the United States can be divided into two groups: Negroes and sensation-mongering Negro leaders. So much is heard from some of the latter that the former are often ignored and more often misunderstood. It creates the impression that the Negro who speaks loudest and most is representative of most Negroes. That, happily for all of us, is not the case.
>
> The Negro that I know, North and South, is not what his agitator-leaders say that he is and want him to be . . . the drive to embitter and unbalance him, which began during the depression under Communist auspices, has gained momentum with American entrance into the war. Nowhere is the drive being so aggressively promoted as in the incendiary columns of the Negro press.
>
> Every incident that can be used to breed ill-will between the races is seized upon . . . in season and out, they present a distorted, dishonest picture of America — and of the progress, place, and opportunity of the Negro in it . . .

Needless to say this comment by Warren Brown did not escape the notice of the Negro newspaperman, and serious students working in this area. The *Saturday Review* gave space for a reply to the article several weeks later.[20] This reply, "What About the Negro Press?" was written by Dr. V. V. Oak of Wilberforce University, a Professor of Sociology and Instructor in Journalism. Among other things Dr. Oak said:

> It is true that the Negro Press is getting more and more militant in its demand for a real democracy at home, but this grow-

---

[18] December 19, 1942.

[19] January, 1943.

[20] March 6, 1942.

ing impatience of the press is quite natural as well as desirable. As a matter of fact, all the non-whites in the world today are demanding greater freedom, and unless the American Negro is entirely unintelligent and unprogressive he is bound to demand his right to be a free American, especially when he is fighting abroad for the preservation of democracy . . .

Academic Interest in the Negro Press. While these more popular articles dealing with the Negro newspaper were getting wide circulation in the nationally syndicated newspaper columns, and in the magazines, another group of academically inclined men were making a sincere effort to understand and interpret the Negro papers in their true perspective. Although these "studies" were in the main subjective, they were conducted in the spirit of scientific inquiry and were free from the emotion and bias that quite obviously colored much of the former type of writing. Their purpose was to understand rather than to discredit or to defend the Negro press.

Even before the current popular interest in the Negro newspapers had arisen, various scholars had come to recognize their potentiality as subjects for sociological investigation. Several articles and at least three books were written on this subject a quarter of a century ago, or earlier.[21] Dr. Frederick G. Detweiler's book, *The Negro Press in the United States,* a cultural

[21] "The Negro Press," in *Annals* of the American Academy of Political and Social Science, CXXXX (Nov., 1928), pp. 248-256; Hershaw, L.M., "Negro Press in America," in *Charities and Commons,* XV (1905) pp. 66-68; Johnson, Charles S., "The Rise of the Negro Magazine," *Journal of Negro History XIII,* No. 1 (1928), pp. 7-21; Gordon, Eugene, "Outstanding Negro Newspapers." *Opportunity,* V. 5 (1927) pp. 358-363; Detweiler, F.G., *The Negro Press in the United States.* (Chicago: University of Chicago Press, 1922); Penn, I. Garland, *The Afro-American Press and Its Editors.* (Springfield, Mass.: Willey and Co., 1891): Kerlin, Robert T., *The Voice of the Negro.* (New York: E.P. Dutton and Co., 1919).

history of Negro newspapers, is the best known of these publications, and is generally accepted even today as the most authoritative source of information on the subject. This publication, originally a doctoral dissertation at the University of Chicago, was written under the direction of the late Robert E. Park, himself a serious student of the sociology of journalism, and author of *The Immigrant Press*. The writer is indebted to both of these students for having stimulated his interest in this area of research.

In a more recent article devoted to the subject, Dr. Detweiler expressed the opinion that "The Negro editor leads his group in being race conscious."[22] Undoubtedly those editors who use such terms as "our group," "race member," or "the race," rather than the racial label, Negro, are doing so to awaken the feeling of "consciousness of kind," or "racial solidarity." There is little question but that race consciousness is promoted and exploited for commercial purposes. In this respect the Negro newspaper plays the dual role of crusading against racial prejudices and discrimination, and yet existing because of the many issues which stem from such attitudes and cultural practices. On this point one editor once said:

> It is agreed that if the black people desire to receive all the benefits of the American Nation they should not seek to build up an independent racial psychology. This is a beautiful altruistic theory, but a theory it is that will not adjust itself to our present condition. As things exist in America, we, the black people, must be self centered and self conscious if we would preserve ourselves.[23]

---

[22] Detweiler, F.G., "The Negro Press Today." *American Journal of Sociology*, XLIV, No. 3 (1938), p. 398.

[23] *The Chicago Whip*, editorial, January 15, 1927.

C. THE HYPOTHESIS

The preceding discussion reveals that much of the popular literature on the Negro press is impressionistic, and frequently biased. The more academic studies, too, have been subjective and qualitative, and lacking in verifiability, although essentially scientific in intent.[24] But it was in the syndicated columns, and widely circulated magazine articles, where the writer fears that there was more heat generated than light thrown on the subject. It was the impact of this popular literature on the American mind that gave rise to this research interest. The writer's concern stems from those frequently voiced and widely circulated allegations that the Negro newspapers are "radical," "communistic," and "subversive."

Even the casual reader must have observed, however, that the Negro newspapers are very critical of many phases of American life. This criticism has been variously interpreted. It is not unusual today to have any criticism of this nation interpreted by some as "subversive" or "communistic." This controversy in the realm of values, between those who defended, and those who attacked the Negro press as "red," motivated this student to seek to frame a hypothesis regarding this matter, that could be stated in objective terms, and tested by quantitative, verifiable methods. The previously mentioned value controversy has been brought into the foreground for the purpose of indicating the source of this research lead, and for pointing up the need for an empirical study of this medium of communication.

---

[24] Kingsbury, Susan M., Hart, Hornell, *Newspapers and the News*, G.P. Putnam's Sons, New York, 1937, p. 88. This study an exception, is based on a space measurement of front page headlines.

Our concern here is not whether the Negro press is "liberal", or "subversive*", in terms of the subjective values of either the critics or the editors. The merits of the research would seem to hinge on whether it can be successfully demonstrated that there are objective criteria in terms of which the political content of these newspapers may be measured, and compared.

We may pose these questions: Are there recognizable symbols which reflect the political ideals and values of historical American society? If so, would not the incidence of attitudes expressed toward these and other political symbols, by the newspapers under discussion, be valid grounds for making inferences regarding the significance of their political content?

Students of American cultural dynamics have spent considerable time in attempting to define the ideal pattern of American society.[25] We may safely assert

---

[25] Beard, Charles A., and Mary, *The American Spirit*. (New York: Macmillan Co., 1942); Becker, Carl, *Freedom and Responsibility in the American Way of Life*. (New York: Alfred A. Knopf, Inc., 1946); Brogan, David W., *The American Character*. (New York: Alfred A. Knopf, Inc., 1944); Croly, Herbert, *The Promise of American Life*. (New York: Macmillan Co., 1909); Curte, Merle, *The Growth of American Thought*. (New York: Harper and Bros., 1943); de Tocqueville, Alexis, *Democracy in America*. (Oxford Univ. Press, Galaxy Edition I Vol., 1947); Hacker, Louis M., *The Shaping of the American Tradition*. (New York: Columbia University Press, 1946); Kluckhohn, Clyde and Florence R., *American Culture: general orientations and class patterns*, 7th Conference of Science, Philosophy and Religion, 1947; Lynd, R.S., *Knowledge For What*. (Princeton University Press, 1939); Myrdal, Gunnar, *An American Dilemma*. (New York: Harper and Bros., 1944); Norton, Thomas J., *The Constitution of the United States*. (New York: America's Future Inc., 1946); Parrington, Vernon L., *Main Currents in American Thought*. (New York: Harcourt Brace and Co., 1930); Rourke, Constance, *The Roots of American Culture*. (New York: Harcourt Brace and Co., 1942); Smith, Bernard, (ed.) *The Democratic Spirit*. (New York: Alfred A. Knopf Inc., 1945); Tyler, Alice F., (ed.) *Freedom's Ferment*. (Minneapolis: University of Minnesota Press, 1944).

that a universe of discourse has emerged in this area. To these students, a meaningful, objective, content is contained in such phrases as "The American democratic tradition," "the democratic spirit," "the American spirit," "the American creed," and the like. To be sure, such phrases are summary statements, constructs, or convenient labels which stand in the place of the complex of values and ideals in our social system. We may by-pass such phrases and go directly to the specific traits for which they stand. Myrdal,[26] for example, says:

> America, compared to every other country in Western Civilization, large or small, has the most explicitly expressed system of ideals in reference to human inter-relations. This body of ideals is more widely understood and appreciated than similar ideals are anywhere else . . . these tenets were written into the Declaration of Independence, the Preamble of the Constitution, the Bill of Rights, and into the Constitutions of the several states.

And what are these tenets of the American creed? Says Ralph Bunch, a distinguished American and scholar:

> Every man in the street, white, black, red, or yellow, knows that this is "the land of the free," the "land of opportunity," the "cradle of liberty," the "home of democracy," that the American flag symbolizes the "equality of all men" and guarantees to us all "the protection of life, liberty and property," "freedom of speech, freedom of religion and racial tolerance."[27]

The American people are conscious of the existence of this subjective ideal patterning of their culture, even though their overt behavior in many situations may seem to be antithetical to their professions. Evidence of this fact is shown by the indignation manifested at

---

[26] Myrdal, Gunnar, *An American Dilemma.*   Harper and Brothers, New York, 1944, pp. 3-4.

[27] *Ibid.*, (quoted) p. 4.

the public opinion level, when incidents arise that can only be interpreted as flagrant violations of the spirit of the liberal democratic creed. When an American Indian, a World War II casualty, was denied burial in a midwestern cemetery reserved for whites only, an outraged public opinion found expression in a Presidential invitation that this dead American soldier be brought to Washington to be buried in the National Cemetery.

When the holder of a winning lottery ticket in a North Carolina town was denied the prize — a Cadillac automobile — because he was a Negro, public indignation was so aroused by this violation of the spirit of fair play and democracy, that one congressman, a member of the Kiwanis Club, one of whose chapters sponsored the raffle, threatened to take the incident to the floor of Congress unless the injustice were speedily rectified.

Because of this serious breach of the spirit of the creed, an otherwise provincial incident was headlined in the daily press, and made the subject of nationwide radio comment. An embarrassed chapter of this national fraternal body was forced, by the pressure of public opinion, to reimburse the holder of the winning ticket — incidentally also a war veteran — in keeping with the rules of the game.

Incidents such as those mentioned here could be multiplied many times. They testify that such phrases as "the democratic spirit," "the American creed," and the like, represent a covert emotional patterning, or predisposition in the American people. These ideals are verbalized in the form of specific symbols which represent the crystallization of the political and social

values on which the nation was founded, and which
serve as mainsprings in motivating the dynamic
cultural process.

The hypothesis being tested here is that this group
of newspapers under consideration reflects the political
ideals and values which are consistent with the liberal
democratic "American Creed," or "the American Tradition."

CHAPTER II

THE METHODOLOGY

A. THE UNIVERSE

An empirical answer to the question as to whether the Negro press in the United States is radical and subversive, or an exponent of the liberal democratic American creed, would necessarily rest on a demonstrated espousal of doctrines alien to, or consistent with these values. The problem is quite apparently one of content analysis. Research procedures in this area are becoming more or less standardized. One approach makes use of some form of space measurement. The other is based on a symbol list which is used as a stable base of comparison. The latter procedure was used in this study.[1]

We are concerned in this analysis with a group of newspapers designated as 'leading' Negro newspapers. Certain specified conditions are imposed as prerequisite to being included in this universe. The newspaper must be listed in a standard newspaper directory, and its circulation verified by a reputable agency. The figures of the Audit Bureau of Circulation are used in

---

[1] The basic methodology employed in this study has been developed by Laswell and Associates. See Laswell, Harold D., "The Politically Significant Content of the Press: Coding Procedures." *Journalism Quarterly*, XIX No. 1, (1942), pp. 12-24; Laswell, Harold D. "The World Attention Survey." *Public Opinion Quarterly*, V No. 4 (1941), pp. 456-62; Davidson, Philip, "An Analysis of the Soviet-Controlled Berlin Press." *Public Opinion Quarterly*, VII, No. 1, (1947), pp. 40-57.

this study. Lastly, in order to be included here, the
weekly circulation must be 50,000 or more copies. This
is, to be sure, an arbitrary figure, but one arrived at
only after a careful study of the audited circulation of
these weeklies had been made. It was found that none
of the papers with a national coverage had a circulation below this figure, and that this group comprised
the most frequently discussed publications among the
critics. One newspaper claiming a circulation of more
than 50,000 copies, but whose figures were not verified
by ABC, was not included in this study.

Turning now to the group of newspapers that meets
our specified criteria, we find that the largest weekly
circulation of any one of them, the *Pittsburgh Courier*,
runs to 296,694,[2] while the one with the smallest circulation, the *Norfolk Journal and Guide*, is 63,028
copies.[3] There are five newspapers in this group. Three
are published in the so-called "balance of power" states
(New York, Illinois and Pennsylvania), one in an
eastern border state (Maryland), the other in the
upper south (Virginia).   These newspapers had a
total circulation of 831,877 copies. This represented
more than 80 percent of the total circulation of the
twenty-two Negro newspapers listed in Ayer and Son's
Directory with an ABC audit. This figure was also
about forty-two percent of the total circulation of the
secular Negro newspapers.

When we turn to a consideration of newspapers
other than those on which our study is based, we find

---

[2] N.W. Ayer and Son. *Directory of Newspapers and Periodicals.*
Philadelphia, Pa., 1949. The selection of 1949 is a methodological
consideration. See section "The Sample." The present circulation is
somewhat smaller.

[3] *Ibid.*

that there is a sharp decline in the certified circulation of those publications. While the median average of the five "leading" weeklies was 189,134 copies, that of the other ABC audited Negro papers was 13,164 copies. All of this would seem to indicate that, at least insofar as circulation is concerned, the newspapers comprising our universe are in a class by themselves. This group constitutes what is known to the Negro newspaperman as "The National Negro Press."[4] They have a nation-wide circulation and are published in national, regional or state, and city editions. They stand in sharp contrast to the smaller papers with local reading publics, and which, if taken individually, would be unknown to the vast majority of Negro readers.

B. THE SAMPLE

Since the present study purports to analyze the political content as of a given time, and is not a study of trends over a period of time, the problem of the sample then is to establish first a base period adequate for a comparative study of the main categories of political content — domestic and foreign. For this purpose, the year 1948 was taken as the period of study. During this year a Presidential election was held, as well as that of many other major elective officials, which fact served to throw the issues and cross-currents of domestic politics into bolder relief. Any consequent increase in the space devoted to political comment, as during an election year, would have no pertinent bearing on our sample since our concern here is not with space measurement, but rather with the attitude ex-

---

[4] The *Amsterdam News*, excepted, is primarily a Metropolitan newspaper.

pressed with reference to certain political symbols. The basis for comparison is the symbol and not the column inch.

During the post-war years Negro newspapers have also had much to say on international and foreign issues, especially where such issues relate to the colored peoples of the world. By 1948 the passions generated by the war had cooled somewhat, while world wide political comment was probably more temperate than is the case today. This period is submitted here as representative of such material appearing in these newspapers.

A random sample was used in the selection of copies of each newspaper for study. Beginning with the second publication issued in January, every third weekly copy for the remainder of the year was read and its political content recorded on an instrument prepared for that purpose. This resulted in a sample of seventeen copies of each newspaper.[5] The split sample technique was applied as a further check on the adequacy of the sample. The positive scores were added for the odd, and even, consecutive issues of each newspaper and summed. This operation gave 54.44 percent positive scores for the odd count and 52.47 percent for the even number. This variability is no more than would be likely to occur in a random sample, since 53.52 percent of the total number of symbols coded had positive scores (See Table VII).

The politically significant content of the newspapers

---

[5] J.L. Woodward, in discussing the problem of adequacy of the sample, held that "a week of six consecutive issues, if carefully selected so as to avoid the biasing effects of 'big news stories'" was sufficient to give stable results. *Foreign News in American Newspapers*, New York: Columbia University Press, 1930. See Chapter II.

under investigation is identified in context by the presence of one or more of the symbols from our basic symbol list which has been shown to have political significance. Symbols in such a list have reference to persons, to groups (i.e., nations and their governmental agencies), or to policies or ideas that are related to the shaping, or implementation of public policy.

The symbols used in this study were primarily based on the list used in "The World Attention Survey" of Laswell and Associates.[6] Other political symbols that were found to appear frequently in these newspapers during trial reading, were added to this list. A basic list of 112 "politically significant" symbols was stabilized with reference to the content of the particular group of papers being studied. While not all of the symbols comprising this list had direct bearing on testing the hypothesis of this study, they were retained and coded when the newspapers were read, since this enabled the writer to gather additional information on the political attitudes of Negro newspapers all in one operation.

The aid of a panel of experts was solicited for the purpose of stablizing a symbol list for testing the hypothesis. This panel was composed of some of the leading students in American sociology, anthropology, and history. All were students of American cultural dynamics. The following methodological note in the form of a letter, was attached to the original symbol list and addressed to each member of the panel:

> The writer is engaged in a study in the area of communications that purports to be an analysis of the politically significant content of a specified group of newspapers. The hypothesis that is being tested is that this group of newspapers under con-

---

[6] Laswell, *op. cit.* pp. 456-62.

sideration reflects the political ideals and values which are consistent with the liberal democratic "American creed," or the "American Tradition."

Because of your recognized standing as a student of American cultural dynamics, you are one of a few experts requested to participate in this enterprise to the extent of aiding in the stabilization of a basic symbol list significant for testing the aforestated hypothesis.

Please score as (+) those symbols which you consider to be consistent with the American creed, and (−) those symbols which are contrary to the creed. Other symbols (for example, Australia) which have no bearing on the American tradition should be given a neutral score (0). If you feel that there are other significant symbols which are not included please write them in and score them.

Eight persons comprised this panel. Agreement of seven of this number, on any symbol, as being significant for testing the hypothesis, was considered to be sufficient for its inclusion in the revised symbol list. This operation resulted in the stabilization of a list of forty-two symbols, twenty of which were considered by the panel to be consistent with the values enunciated by the American creed, and twenty-two of which were opposed to those values. (See appendix II.)

C. CODING

Each symbol is scored in keeping with the manner in which it is presented in context. When presented in a favorable light it is given a positive (+) score; when presented in an unfavorable light it is given a negative (−) score. Other presentations are neutral. As a check on the reliability of the writers' scoring, a sample of articles was submitted to a group of lay judges for scoring. The logic in the selection of laymen was that the newspapers are addressed to the general reader rather than to the expert. The reaction of the layman then, in the coding of political symbols, should prove a more valid basis for comparison of scoring than that of the hypercritical professional.

The primary concern in the selection of items for coding was to insure a spread of items over the three sections of the newspapers being considered, namely, the personal columns, news, and editorial section. There was an attempt made to obtain a representative distribution of symbols in the items read. The only other consideration was for the time required of the volunteer participants.

Of the seven persons[7] who agreed to take part, one score sheet had to be discarded because quite obviously there was a misunderstanding of the instructions. The material to be coded, together with the score sheets, were left with the respondent, and instructions were given at that time. The score sheets were called for after the coding had been completed since this operation consumes a considerable amount of time. Only in one case was the investigator present when the scoring was done.

Each panel member coded the symbols in a news story, an editorial, and a personal column, for a combined total of 138 scores. Of this number of individual judgments, 126 matched those of the investigator. Stated in percentages, 91.3 percent of the scores of the panel matched those of the investigator. There were no absolute contradictions, the margin of variation being in the neutral category.

---

[7] In this group, two were College instructors, although not in Social Sciences; two were High School teachers, one an English teacher, the other an instructor in Commercial subjects. One participant was a State employee, with college training; another an undergraduate English major; and a housewife, also a college graduate, completed the group.

We are not, however, making a study of total newspaper space. A restricted rather than an inclusive base of comparison seemed to be more practical since it can be demonstrated upon examination, that most of the politically significant content is to be found in the three following departments: news stories, editorials, and the personal columns. Our study is confined to these sections even though some of the symbols may appear in other departments of the newspapers — in such features as letters to the editor, the roving reporter, fiction, paid political advertisements, quotations from other newspapers, society news and the like. Similarly, cartoons, comics and other drawings, which admittedly may have political import, are not included in this study since we have as yet no reliable technique for equating the space-meaning relevance of such features with the unit-symbol base used here.

A distinction is made here between domestic and foreign political content. "Foreign News" is identified by its source of origin from outside the United States, as for example London, Johannesburg, South Africa, or Buenos Aires. Foreign news, then is to be distinguished from news features about foreign countries which are of domestic origin.

The basic unit of comparison in this study is the article. Other units such as the sentence, or paragraph, are theoretically possible, but it appeared after a close survey of many copies of these newspapers, that the use of a smaller "specified context" — i.e., that portion of the text to be read in determining how the symbol is presented — than the article, would neither be necessary, nor justify the additional time required in working with a smaller base.

The "recording unit" made use of in this research

is likewise the article. By recording unit is meant the range of text for which a symbol is tabulated with the unit weight of one, even though the symbol may occur more than once in the given range of text. This, of course, is another way of saying that we are using a weighted symbol list, and that, in our basic unit, the article, each politically significant symbol is scored only once. Thus the symbol presented in each specified context, whether favorable or unfavorable, is tabulated with the unit weight of one.

CHAPTER III

THE POLITICAL CONTENT AND
THE AMERICAN CREED

A. GENERAL ORIENTATION

While in the process of coding the politically significant content of the five leading Negro newspapers
used as the basis of this study, the writer scored a
total of 10,195 symbols. The absolute number of symbols coded is shown in Table I, cross-classified by
newspaper and by score. The Pittsburgh *Courier* contained the largest number of political symbols with
2,588 and the New York *Amsterdam News,* a tabloid,
the fewest with 981 symbols.

TABLE I. NUMBER OF POLITICALLY SIGNIFICANT
SYMBOLS BY NEWSPAPER AND SCORE

Paper	Total	Positive (+)	Negative (−)	Neutral (0)
Courier[1]	2,588	977	1,041	570
Afro-American	2,240	954	744	542
Journal & Guide[2]	1,888	843	588	457
Amsterdam News	981	399	334	248
Defender	2,498	1,046	948	504
Total	10,195	4,219	3,655	2,321

[1] Figures are based on a sample of 14 copies.
[2] Figures are based on a sample of 16 copies; all other samples are
based on 17 copies.

These symbols were distributed in 2,370 separate
items, or articles as shown in the following Table:

TABLE II. NUMBER OF ARTICLES READ BY NEWSPAPER
AND SECTION

Paper	Total	News			Opinion		
		Total	Domestic	Foreign	Total	Editorials	Columns
Courier	466	338	315	23	128	38	90
Afro-American	581	468	427	41	113	58	55
Journal & Guide	485	394	363	31	91	36	55
Amsterdam News	233	179	166	13	54	21	33
Defender	605	380	347	33	225	60	165
Total	2,370	1,759	1,618	141	611	213	398

A mean average of 4.30 symbols per item is obtained. There was some variation from this when the three sections of the newspapers being analyzed were considered separately. The personal columns average 6.82 political symbols per column, the editorials 5.79 symbols, and the news items averaged 3.55 symbols per item.

CHART I. AVERAGE NUMBER OF POLITICALLY SIGNIFICANT SYMBOLS PER ITEM BY SECTIONS

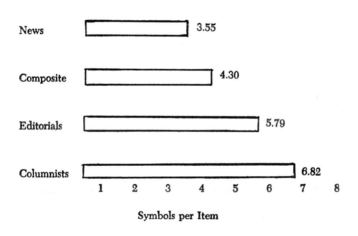

Symbols per Item

An examination of the percentage distribution of scored symbols reveals that, on the whole, there is a favorable balance in the treatment of news and opinion as manifested in the ratio of positive or favorable, over negative or unfavorable scores. The percentage distribution of scores is presented in Table III.

TABLE III.   PERCENTAGE DISTRIBUTION OF POLITICALLY
SIGNIFICANT SYMBOLS BY NEWSPAPER AND SCORE

Paper	Total	Positive (+1)	Negative (−1)	Neutral (0)
Courier	25.38	37.75	40.22	22.03
Afro-American	21.97	42.58	33.21	24.21
Journal & Guide	18.51	44.64	31.14	24.20
Amsterdam News	9.62	40.67	34.04	25.28
Defender	24.50	41.87	37.95	20.17
Total	99.98	41.38	35.85	22.76

As shown here 41.38 percent of the total symbols
scored were given positive scores, and 35.85 were
negative scores. The remaining scores were neutral.
Only among the columnists is there to be found a
somewhat higher percentage of negative scores as
shown in the Table that follows:

TABLE IV.   PERCENTAGE DISTRIBUTION OF POLITICALLY
SIGNIFICANT SYMBOLS BY SECTION AND SCORE

Section	Total	Positive (+1)	Negative (−1)	Neutral (0)
News	61.26	42.85	33.23	23.90
Columns	26.64	36.08	40.20	23.71
Editorials	12.09	45.58	39.49	14.92
Total	99.99	41.38	35.85	22.76

In this department of these newspapers, 40.20 percent of all politically significant symbols were scored
negatively, while 36.08 percent were given a positive
score. But in the editorial section, all-important for
determining the policy and tone of the newspaper,
and in the news items, together constituting approximately 75 percent of all symbols coded, there is a

higher incidence of positive scores. The editorial section shows the highest percentage of positive scores with 45.58 followed by the news items with 42.85. The percentages of negative scores were 39.49 and 33.23 respectively.

On the basis of the greater frequency of occurrence of positive, or favorable scores we feel justified in concluding that these newspapers as a group are essentially constructive,[3] and represent a positive force in the presentation of material out of which opinion is molded.

Variations in the presentation of symbols among the three categories of the newspaper being examined, and among the newspapers themselves deserve further comment. Nearly two-thirds (61.26 percent) of all coded symbols were to be found in the news items. (See Table IV) The personal columns followed with 26.64 percent, and last came the editorial section with 12.09 percent of the political symbols. There is some deviation from these composite percentages, when individual newspapers are considered, that is significant for understanding the policy and emphasis of the different publications.

In the *Afro-American*, for example, approximately 75 percent of the political symbols were to be found in the news items. This same paper is last in the percentage of symbols found among its columnists with 13.97 percent, and stands at the median in the

---

[3] Constructive, as used here, is a quantitative construct based on a higher incident of (+), or positive, scores. It is meant to indicate that a particular newspaper stands "for" something, or some things, as demonstrated statistically, to a greater degree than it registers protest or opposition to something, or some things. This construct is not meant to include an evaluation of the things advocated or opposed.

editorial department with 11.69 percent. Quite apparently the chief emphasis given the political content in the *Afro* is on news coverage. Quantitatively, the political writing among its columnists lags far behind that of the other newspapers studied. (See Table XI, Appendix II Tables)

The *Defender*, on the other hand, is particularly strong in political opinion. More than half of the political symbols coded, 52.39 percent, were found in its personal columns and in its editorials. (See Table VIII) The *Defender* is also the most opinionated of these newspapers, as indicated by the smallest percentage of neutral scores. (See Table IX) As compared with the other newspapers, a larger percentage (27 percent) of its articles were personal columns, as shown in Table V, and a larger percentage of all political symbols were found in this department, with 37.71 percent. (See Table XI)

TABLE V.   PERCENTAGE DISTRIBUTION OF ARTICLES
READ BY PAPER AND SECTION

Paper	Total	News			Opinion		
		Total	Domestic	Foreign	Total	Editorials	Columns
Courier	19.66	72.53	93.19	6.80	27.46	8.15	19.31
Afro-American	24.51	80.55	91.23	8.76	19.44	9.98	9.46
Journal & Guide	20.46	81.23	92.13	7.86	18.76	7.42	11.34
Amsterdam News	9.83	76.82	92.73	7.26	23.17	9.01	14.16
Defender	25.52	62.81	91.31	8.68	37.18	9.91	27.27
Total	99.98	74.21	91.98	8.01	25.77	8.98	16.79

This emphasis given political opinion in the *Defender*, bears out quantitatively the statement of policy made by its founder and editor, the late Robert S. Abbott, when he said that he founded his paper on the theory that his people would support anyone who would take the lead in the fight for complete equality and justice. "I believe today as I have always believed," he said, "that a Negro newspaper can survive only so long as it adheres to this policy."[4]

The Pittsburgh *Courier* follows the *Defender* in all three of the last mentioned particulars. It is the second most opinionated newspaper with the second largest number of personal columns, and has the second largest percentage of political symbols found in this section with 32.57 percent. The *Courier* leads all other newspapers in this universe, however, with the largest number of symbols per item. (See Table XII)

The *Courier* is unique in that it alone shows a higher percentage of negative than of positive scores, with 40.22 and 37.75 percentages respectively. (See Table III) This negativism is particularly pronounced among its columnists where 44.96 percent of the political symbols coded were negative, as compared with 32.50 percent having positive scores. (See Table XIII) This represents the highest incidence of negativism to be found in any department among these leading newspapers, and in all probability in the entire Negro press.

The Norfolk *Journal and Guide* is second to the *Afro* in straight reporting of political news, and in de-emphasizing political opinion. (See Table XI) More than 70 percent of the political symbols coded were

---

[4] Quoted in Jones, Dewey Roscoe, "Effects of the Negro Press on Race Relations in the South," Masters Thesis, Columbia University, New York, 1932, p. 3.

found in its news items. The median for the group was 58.41 percent.

The *Journal and Guide* leads all the other newspapers studied in the percentage of positive scores, with a composite figure for all departments of 44.64 percent. (See Table III) Its editorial section is particularly constructive with 52.23 percent of its political symbols being scored positively. (See Table XIV)

The columnists, too, show a higher percentage of positive than of negative scores with 45.53 and 32.96 percent respectively. This is not true of the columnists of any other newspapers in this group. (See Table XIII) The *Courier* columnists' scores by comparison registered the highest percentage of protest symbols with 44.96 percent negative scores. It would seem that the columnists of the *Journal and Guide* are less given to negative criticism than are the columnists in the other newspapers studied.

The New York *Amsterdam News,* the only tabloid in this group of newspapers, is primarily a community newspaper serving the greater New York area. One divergent feature of some significance is its slightly higher percentage of political symbols, 15.08 percent, found in the editorial section. (See Table XI) By way of comparison, it is followed by the *Defender* with its strong editorial emphasis, with 14.68 percent of all coded political symbols. The editorial comment of the *Amsterdam News* is particularly constructive, 50.67 percent of the scores being given a positive code. In this respect it is second only to the *Journal and Guide* with 52.23 percent positive scores. The percentage of negative scores in the editorial section is the lowest of any of these newspapers. The *Amsterdam News* is characterized by a vigorous, constructive editorial section.

More than 2,300 items (See Table II) were read and their political symbols coded by the writer, nearly 75 percent of which were news items. The remaining items were opinion, and were distributed between personal columns, 16.79 percent, and editorials, 8.98 percent. (See Table V)

The *Defender,* with 37 percent of its items in the opinion category, was a standout in this respect. The *Journal and Guide* and the *Afro,* each with more than 80 percent news items, led in this area. Both of the latter newspapers were below the median in the percentage of opinion articles.

News items were classified into two sub-categories, domestic and foreign, the latter originating from a source outside the United States. Eight percent of the news items were of foreign origin. This may be compared roughly with seven percent foreign news (by space measurement) carried in seven leading metropolitan dailies in the United States.[5] The percentage of foreign news, however, is a very unstable category since changes in the international situation, such as periods of tension, or war, will have a direct bearing on news interest abroad. During World War II, when these newspapers had their own war correspondents covering the major battle areas, the percentage of foreign news would have been much higher.

Highlights of editorial opinion on various aspects of domestic and international politics are presented in the following paragraphs. Since each political symbol is scored only once in a given item, the number of scores for each symbol represents the number of editorials in which that symbol is coded.

---

[5] Bird, George L., and Merwin, Frederic E., *The Newspaper and Society.* New York: Prentice-Hall, Inc., 1949, p. 111.

These newspapers unanimously support the symbol "American Tradition," the editorial count being eight favorable, with none in opposition. They likewise favored the American people, five favorable editorials to two unfavorable; but registered disapproval of America as a social system, 26 to 10.

Although four of the five newspapers in this group supported the Republican Party in the 1948 election, yet they were unfavorable to the Republican dominated 80th Congress, 3 editorials to 1. Dewey got a vote of confidence 9-1, but the Republican Party ran into considerable unfavorable comment, although winning out on the long end of a 13-8 editorial count. Mr. Republican, the late Senator Robert Taft, and the Taft-Hartley Bill, got approval 5-3.

President Truman won out in the battle of the editorials by a wide margin 29-13. The number of editorials in which his name appeared in our sample also made him the most popular and controversial political figure. The Democratic Party, too, made a good showing with a 9-8 favorable score, especially so when we consider that, with a single exception, these newspapers were officially supporting the Republican Party.

The Southern wing of the Democratic Party (coded: Southern Democrats), however, with a 15-0 unfavorable count, takes severe criticism in these newspapers. The Dixiecrats lose 9-0; the South, as a region, loses the editorial battle 59-2; while the Southerners who inhabit the region, came out on the short end of a 29-2 count.

Henry Wallace and his Progressive Party were rejected 8-3. The three favorable editorials were on Mr. Wallace. There were none for his party.

The North, gets a shaky vote of confidence 4-3 and

the N.A.A.C.P. gets full support 5-0. All of the editorials favored peace, 10-0, and rejected war 13-1. They also treated the New Deal unfavorably, one editorial to three, to round out the picture of domestic politics.

On the world scene these leading Negro newspapers favor internationalism — the United Nations and the Marshall Plan getting the unanimous endorsement of the twelve editorials in which these symbols were coded.

Latin America, too, was given unanimous approval 4-0. The liberal racial policies in the Latin countries usually get favorable comment in the Negro newspapers.

Russia is rejected in editorial opinion by a six to one count.

Great Britain does not fare much better, the score being five to two against the Island Kingdom. The "Empire taint" undoubtedly was the decisive factor against that country.

The Jews are given favorable comment 6-1, while opinion is divided on Zionism as a movement, 2-2.

In spite of the general liberal leaning of these newspapers, one cannot fail to observe marked traces of conservatism in certain areas. Four of the five publications supported the Republican Party in the 1948 election. Only one officially supported Mr. Truman and the Fair Deal Program. Comment on the President, however, was in the main favorable, due chiefly to his stand on civil rights. As was stated previously, the Progressive Party of Mr. Wallace was rejected in editorial opinion. One columnist was dropped by one of these newspapers when he continued to write favorably of this movement. Senator Taft and the Taft-Hartley Bill, were given official approval in the majority of editorials, although there was a "dragging of the feet."

B. THE PRESS AND THE CREED

It may be recalled that this inquiry was undertaken in order to examine more closely a certain kind of thinking regarding Negro newspapers; more specifically, to examine the view that they were "radical," "subversive" and "communistic." The hypothesis underlying the investigation was that they were indigenous in their orientation, rather than alien to the American Tradition. As stated earlier, in order to test this hypothesis the panel of experts (See Chapter II, Methodology) was asked to select from the original list of 112 political symbols those that were consistent with the "American tradition," and those that were contrary to it. The group participating in the stabilization of this basic symbol list, was composed of social scientists whose names are closely associated with the literature in the area of American cultural dynamics. They agreed on a list of forty-two symbols, twenty of which were consistent with the creed, and twenty-two of which opposed this set of values. (See Table XVIII) This section of the report concerns itself with an analysis of the findings.

The revised symbol list was isolated and the original codes checked off on a second instrument for a closer scrutiny, and were then tabulated. The three sections — news, personal columns, and editorials, remained the basic categories under which the scores were classified. There were over five thousand separate tabulations of these symbols. Table VI shows the absolute numerical distribution of these symbols, by newspaper and by score.

TABLE VI. NUMBER OF SYMBOLS BY PAPER AND SCORE
SIGNIFICANT FOR AMERICAN CREED

Paper	Total	Positive (+1)	Negative (−1)	Neutral (0)
Courier	1,245	610	510	125
Afro-American	1,120	610	401	109
Journal & Guide	946	548	316	82
Amsterdam News	474	234	203	37
Defender	1,224	679	458	87
Total	5,009	2,681	1,888	440

When the percentages of favorable, unfavorable and
neutral scores, of the symbol list having to do with the
American Creed, are compared with corresponding
percentages based on the original symbol list, significant changes in the percentages of these codes are apparent. The composite percentage of positive scores
rose from 41.38 percent of the total, to 53.52 percent.
There was a decrease in neutral scores from 22.76 percent to 8.78 percent. (See Tables III, VII) The percentage of negative scores remained virtually the same.

TABLE VII. PERCENTAGE OF SYMBOLS BY PAPER
AND SCORE SIGNIFICANT FOR AMERICAN CREED

Paper	Total	Positive (+1)	Negative (−1)	Neutral (0)
Courier	24.85	48.99	40.96	10.04
Afro-American	22.35	54.46	35.80	9.73
Journal & Guide	18.88	57.93	33.39	8.66
Amsterdam News	9.48	49.36	42.82	7.80
Defender	24.43	55.47	37.41	7.10
Total	99.99	53.52	37.69	8.78

One may infer from these figures that, where these Negro journalists express themselves with reference to those values which lie at the core of American culture, their writing is more constructive, their views more positive, and that they are less inclined to be neutral, or to compromise.

When the revised symbol list is cross classified by section — news, editorial, columnists — and by score, the findings lend support to the validity of our previous inferences. There is a marked increase in the percentage of positive scores in each of these categories, and the same corresponding decrease in neutral scores. (See Table XVI) Where the historical values underlying our society are concerned, the columnists too, who had previously been characterized by their negativism, show a significantly higher incidence of positive scores, an increase from 36.08 percent to 52.18 percent.

Editorial comment is sharp and constructive with more than 60 percent positive scores. The percentage of neutral scores is the lowest for any category in the study, the figure being 4.37 percent. It becomes obvious, then, from the distribution of coded symbols, that political comment is more direct and less ambiguous when attention is directed toward those political symbols that relate to the American value scheme.

If the number of occurrences of a given symbol in a specified sample is an indication of the emphasis intended — and all such quantitative studies operate on the assumption that such is the case — then the identification of these newspapers with subversive, or communistic political leanings, is not sustained. One fact that stands out is the relative infrequency of occurrence of such symbols. By selecting from the list those symbols which may be considered subversive, and red, (anarchy, Bolshevism, communism, Stalin) it is found that the entire group is scored only 210 times. If this is meant to be a point of emphasis it is unimpressive, when we consider that in all over five thousand scores were recorded. Protest against discrimination and segregation, for example, both of which are likewise considered to be contrary to the creed, accounted for over eleven-hundred scores.

It is when we compare the percentages of favorable and unfavorable scores, with reference to the alleged communistic leanings of these newspapers, that it becomes even more apparent that this view is lacking in demonstrable evidence. Only 6.19 percent of such scores were favorable to the "red" symbols, while 55.19 percent were unfavorable to those symbols.

We may then raise the question basic to our study. If, as the evidence indicates, the view that there is an identification of this group of newspapers with communism, is, to say the least, an uninformed point of view;[6] then does the evidence sustain the hypothesis underlying this study? It is still necessary to inquire whether these newspapers reflect the political ideals and values which are consistent with the liberal democratic American tradition.

The answer to this question would necessarily hinge, or so it would seem, on the consistency in the scoring of those symbols which reflect the historical values of American culture, and likewise those symbols alien to it.

---

[6] Mr. Thomas W. Young, President of the Negro Publishers Assn., in an address to Alpha Phi Alpha Fraternity in Tulsa, Okla., Dec. 1947, defended the capitalistic system as "The best the world has yet produced" and suggested caution in the whole advocacy of any other economic system.

As shown here, those symbols reflecting the values of American society were coded nearly three-thousand times. (See Table XVIII) Eighty-eight percent of these scores were positive or favorable to these symbols, while 2.95 percent were negative. (See Table XIX) Since the positive score is an index of approval, we can only conclude that these newspapers give their overwhelming endorsement to the set of values underlying the ideal pattern of the American social order. They are the same values that are being discussed in the news and are being advocated with considerable heat in the sections of opinion.

But if these newspapers give their unqualified support to the ideal pattern of American democratic society, they reject with equal vehemence some of the prevailing sets of relationships which constitute the real pattern. In speaking for a racial minority, they are particularly critical of the denial to this minority of citizenship rights applicable to other men. It is apparently this criticism of the discrepancy between the ideal pattern and the real — the things America professes, and the things it does — that has brought them to the attention of many public figures, and has aroused in some considerable resentment, and charges of communism. In the order of frequency of occurrence of the respective symbols (See Table XVIII), these newspapers speak out for civil liberties, equality, the franchise, democracy, the Supreme Court and the Constitution. They register their disapproval of segregation, discrimination, racism, communism, and the poll tax.

CHAPTER IV

NEWS IN THE NEGRO NEWSPAPER

A. THE SUPPLEMENTAL FUNCTION

The role of the Negro press is essentially that of a supplemental press. The day by day reporting of the news is followed by colored people in the dailies and other mass media of communication. But for those news stories which hold special interest for them, they eagerly await the appearance of their own newspapers for the story behind the news, to see "what really happened." These newspapers usually oblige by presenting the news and other features with the colored reader solely in mind. They abstract from the mass of news gathered during the week those items of special and timely interest to Negroes, enlarge them, and redefine them from their own viewpoint. There is consequently a tendency to featurize the news, and to interpret it in the light of the readers' interests. This is exactly what the Negro public has come to expect of its press.[1] It wants to know, how, as a minority group, it may be affected by something that has taken place, or is likely to take place. This is a feature, however, that all minority publications have in common. This is their

---

[1] Eighty-six percent of Negroes polled in a nation wide survey replied "yes" in answer to the question "Does the Negro Press speak for most Negroes in its opinions?" Ten percent answered "no," while four percent were undecided. Reported by Lee, Wallace, "Does The Negro Press Speak For Most Negroes?" *Negro Digest,* February 1943, p. 54.

chief *raison d'etre* and should be evaluated in this light.

Some critics of Negro newspapers have spoken of the supplemental function of the Negro newspapers in a derogatory manner. They have tended to evaluate the content of these journals by the standards of news interest which prevail in the white dailies. The Negro papers are addressed to a different public, and this "race angling" the news, as Mr. Pegler calls it, is quite a normal function in view of their special interests. This characteristic is shared by all minority publications, racial, national or religious.

Many white dailies have recognized the existence of the need for greater news coverage in the Negro community, and have included one or more columns of "Negro news" or, "Colored Activities." While the columns are read with interest by many colored subscribers, they fail to meet the special demands of Negro news interest. These news items are local in character and relate mainly to social activities of the churches, clubs and societies, and human interest features. Controversial themes are taboo, and national and international events of primary concern to colored people are not to be found in these columns.

In some Southern cities a few white dailies have developed the practice of publishing a special "black star" edition for distribution in the Negro neighborhoods. The financial page is likely to be deleted and the space given over to news and features relating to the affairs of the Negro community. But, as in the case of those newspapers carrying a column of "Colored Activities," the news is chiefly local with some news items devoted to topics of general national interest to Negroes. The Negro viewpoint is not presented, however, as in the Negro newspapers, nor is the news coverage as extensive.

Many events in which Negroes have figured in a creditable manner would go unnoticed if these facts were not culled out, and pointed up, by the Negro newspapers. When members of their race acquit themselves with distinction in various fields of endeavor, the Negro people want to read about it, and this usually calls for a bigger story than the white daily is likely to give them. Many feel, however, that these same white papers all too frequently play up news that reflects discredit on the Negro people. On this point, one well informed student wrote: ". . . the daily paper as a rule, carries little or no information about doings of Negroes other than that which is criminal or comical. If he wishes to translate those national events into terms of his own people . . . he must turn to the special papers published for the specific purpose of giving him that information."[2]

When young Dean Dixon becomes the first Negro to conduct a major symphony orchestra in Carnegie Hall, colored people want to know more about the event than the barest mention of the fact in white newspapers — if mentioned at all.

When, after the attack on Pearl Harbor, word leaked out that a Negro messman, one Dorie Miller, stationed on a warship there, who had never been permitted to get combat training in the navy, had manned a machine gun and turned it upon the attacking Japanese planes, Negro people wanted to read more about it in their newspapers. Following the persistent efforts of these

[2] Barnett, Claude, A., (Director, Associated Negro Press) "Negro Press Important Arm of Nation at War." Radio Address, Columbia Broadcasting System, March 7, 1942. Reprinted in Norfolk *Journal and Guide,* March 14, 1942.

newspapers, Miller eventually got a medal of honor, and the Negro people a hero.

Newsworthy, too, were the exploits of combat troops in both World Wars. World War I provided an opportunity for blending important news and race promotion on a big scale, and stimulated the development of Negro career journalists. The white dailies were too concerned with the broader aspects of the war to satisfy the special interests of various minority groups involved. The concern of American Negroes for news relating to their relatives and friends in the armed forces could only be satisfied by the Negro newspapers. During the last war all of the major Negro newspapers[3] had their own accredited war correspondents in the various theaters of operation.

A recurrent news theme in the Negro papers has been the contrasts in the patterns of social relationships which developed between American Negro troops and the peoples of the European countries, and those existing at home. The acceptance of the Negro as a social equal in England, France, and, more recently, in Germany has been a focal point of friction between Negro and white troops. The latter have frequently been accused of spreading American race prejudice in those countries where it had not been evident.[4]

---

[3] From the opening of the war to 1946, the *Chicago Defender* had five foreign correspondents; the *Journal and Guide* had five; the *Afro-American* had eight; the *Pittsburgh Courier* had eight. Oak, V.V., *The Negro Newspaper.* Yellow Springs, Ohio: Antioch College Press, 1948, p. 40.

[4] Among other things, it was reported in various Negro papers during the recent war that white soldiers were telling the Nationals of the European countries that Negro soldiers had tails. Conversations with many Negro soldiers by the writer has substantiated the existence of this widely circulated rumor.

Some white publications have likewise taken cognizance of this theme.[5]

The bulk of the news found in the Negro newspapers, however, is of domestic origin. Any news of an interracial nature always has reader appeal, whether Negroes are directly involved, or are affected by events over which they have no personal control. The following dispatches indicate items of the latter type.

F.E.P.C. Made Issue
In Georgia Election

Wrightsville, Ga. Jan. 31, (1948). — Voters and candidates in a primary election in Johnson County must sign pledges stating that they favor the white primary and racial segregation and oppose the F.E.P.C. and Communism.

W.C. Brinson, Chairman of the county's democratic committee, said last week that voters must sign the pledge before they will be allowed to cast a ballot, and candidates must sign it before they can qualify to run.

Heretofore, Democratic executive committees in Georgia have required only a pledge to support nominees as a requirement for primary voting . . .[6]

Miss. Students Insulted At
Governor's Open House

Jackson, Miss. Jan. 31, (1948). — Twelve students and instructors from Jackson College who lined up with other guests in front of the Executive Mansion to felicitate Gov. and Mrs. Fielding L. Wright, during an inaugural open house last week, walked away when a State patrolman "steered them to the back of the mansion."[7]

N.A.A.C.P. Fights Race Baiting
in Loyalty Test

New York, Nov. 20 (1948). — Charging that officials in certain government agencies are using the President's loyalty order as an instrument for intimidating federal employees who oppose dis-

[5] *Newsweek*, September 16, 1946.
[6] *Afro-American*, January 31, 1948.
[7] *Afro-American*, January 31, 1948.

crimination and segregation, the National Association for the Advancement of Colored People has announced a decision by the Association's board of directors to defend accused federal workers in cases where the charges are based on race or color, membership in the N.A.A.C.P., or membership or activity in any coordinating group approved by the Association's national office . . . In Cleveland alone 20 postal workers have been brought up on charges. . . . If the present trend continues, the resolution asserts, "not one of the more than 150,000 colored government employees throughout the country will be safe.[8]

The foregoing are but a few examples of this type of news item to be found in almost any Negro newspaper. Many reports show considerably less restraint, as in cases of violence. While much of this news never finds its way into the white press, such reports of discriminatory treatment of members of the race are of primary concern to Negro people everywhere. Such news furnishes the raw material for the editorials and personal columns. In the opinion sections, such occurrences are likely to be discussed with considerable feeling, in which it is recurrently pointed out that the failure of the American nation to deal fairly with its racial minorities is the real test of its democratic professions. One interesting response to such criticism that has developed of late, has been a disposition to charge the Negro newspapers with disloyalty. Those who make this charge claim that, by playing up such incidents, these newspapers give the enemies of our democracy a powerful propaganda weapon.

Not all of the news in the Negro newspapers is controversial, however. Here, too, is the only adequate record kept of the cultural life of the Negro people. Without these journals there would be little information available concerning their educational institutions,

---

[8] *Journal and Guide,* November 20, 1948.

their churches, their business activities and fraternal affairs.   Here, too, is the Negroes' record of achievement.   The exceptional men and women of the race who have done well against the odds, find a prominent place in the pages of these publications.   In the professions and in politics the race is represented by men whose contributions are significant by any standards. Such names as the late Drs. Charles Drew, who developed the blood bank, and George Washington Carver, the research chemist, were world known.   Similarly, in political life Dr. Ralph Bunche, Federal Judge William Hastie, Congressmen William Dawson and Adam Clayton Powell, are men of distinction in their respective areas.   There are many other less well known, but successful persons in these areas, whose achievements, and social activities are a constant source of news interest to the Negro reading public.

The opening of organized sports, particularly major league baseball and professional football, to Negro athletes, has stimulated interest in the sports section of these Negro newspapers.   The net effect has been to give the sports writers a psychological lift, and to provide a selling point at the news stands.   The standard of writing in the sports department among the major papers is high.

Considerable space is devoted to news of stage, screen, and the musical world.   In the world of entertainment, world famous artists such as Dean Dixon, a composer and major symphony conductor, Marian Anderson, Duke Ellington, Paul Robeson, Katherine Dunham, and others, share space indiscriminately with little known exponents of some new musical innovation.   Although colorful and vibrant, the theatrical and entertainment section in the Negro papers is poorly handled from a technical point of view. Responsible criticism in this area is almost non-existent. The reader is introduced to an undifferentiated array of performers of all sorts, who have just completed "successful engagements" at various places of entertainment.

Another development of considerable interest to one reading public of the Negro newspapers, has been the expansion of the Society news department. Colored people, as do all people, like to see themselves presented in favorable circumstances. The activities of Negro Club women, weddings, and other social gatherings among Negroes, are of little interest to the white dailies, but are as vital to the lives of colored people as similar news in the metropolitan dailies is to their white readers.[9] A glance at this section may prove interesting and informative to those unfamiliar with this phase of Negro life. The somewhat separate life which Negro people in the United States are forced to live may have resulted, as is frequently alleged, in over-compensation in the treatment of society news in these newspapers.

B.   SENSATIONALISM IN THE NEWS

News of a more sensational nature also finds its place in Negro newspapers. While there is considerable difference in the emphasis given this kind of material by various publications, a common recurrent criticism of the Negro papers has been the sensational character of a considerable portion of the front page news. It may be easily verified, by inspection of a few copies,

---

[9] Some dailies with considerable circulation in Negro neighborhoods have carried a full page of Negro news and features for distribution in those neighborhoods. This page was not included in those papers intended for general circulation.

that stories treating crime, murder, love triangles, police brutality, sex, the doings of racketeers, and such, are given considerable space. While the prominence of such material will be found to vary in different journals, the idea is rather widespread that the Negro press devotes too much attention to "scandals."

The Negro newspapermen are aware of the criticism of sensationalism. This feature is not original with them, having been adopted from the Hearst newspapers, and consciously pursued for the purpose of extending circulation. One columnist,[10] at least, manages to clothe the practice with a noble aim. She says:

> We confess it (sensationalism) to be deliberate bait earnestly employed in the hope that the readers will be attracted and then will stay with us long enough to recognize the serious message that is the burden of our business.

Myrdal, however, feels that the main reason why the Negro press "exaggerates the American pattern of sensational journalism" is that the Negro community, compared with the white world, is so predominantly lower class.[11]

Be that as it may, Kingsbury and Hart, in a study of sensationalism, found that the Negro newspapers "gave less attention on the average to sex interest than did the white tabloids."[12] Their findings were based on a comparative study of the percentages of front page headline space devoted to sex. The *Chicago Defender* was found to be the most sensational of the Negro papers, and the *New York Age* the least. Both the New York *Mirror* and the *Daily News*, however, were

[10] Marjorie McKenzie, *Pittsburgh Courier*, January 10, 1948.

[11] Myrdal, *op. cit.*, p. 917; See also Burma, *op. cit.*, p. 177.

[12] Kingsbury, and Hart. *op. cit.*, p. 88.

more sensational than the *Defender*. The *Age* was in a class with such papers as the Cleveland *Plain Dealer*, a white daily, in which sensational news was not prominent.

It may well be that Langston Hughes, columnist for the *Chicago Defender*, has the best answer to the charge of sensationalism of them all. To him it is merely a case of factual reporting on what happened. He says:

> . . . what is Negro life in this rough-and-tumble America of ours if not sensational? What is life in the black ghettoes — Harlem, Chicago's South Side, Auburn Avenue, Rampart Street — if not sensational. What is Congress with its Rankins and Eastmans, or the Army with its Royals, or politics with its racial and regional splits, if not sensational?[13]

Sensationalism in the American press is an urban development and as previously stated is not confined to the Negro newspaper. Sensational news is made in the city environment with its highly mobile and heterogeneous populations. The extent to which such copy finds its way into various newspapers is a matter of editorial policy. Such newspapers as the New York *Times* and the *Herald Tribune* give little space to this kind of news. The main source of their revenue is advertisement. Their publics are more intellectually inclined. Other newspapers, however, such as the *News* and *Mirror*, both of which are published in the same city, have much larger circulations which they have built up by catering to a more elemental whim of mass man who would "rather be entertained than edified," as the late Robert E. Park once phrased it.[14] The

---

[13] From column "Here to Yonder," *Chicago Defender*, June 26, 1948.
[14] Hughes, Helen M., *News and The Human Interest Story*. Chicago: University of Chicago Press, 1939. "Introduction."

difficulties which the Negro newspapers have encoun-
tered in obtaining advertising has likewise led them to
maximize sales, sensational news being one among other
resources exploited in the process.

It would be a mistake to regard the larger Negro
newspapers as provincial, even though they are weeklies
and are addressed to a racial minority with a relatively
high rate of illiteracy. While they may be compared
with the country weeklies in regard to the supplemental news function, they show a cosmopolitan outlook that is foreign to the white country weekly. They
are products of the metropolitan region and reflect its
intellectual climate. The main centers of news development both at home and abroad, are tapped by the staff
writers and correspondents of the larger Negro papers.
In this respect they tend to approach the scope of news
coverage of the metropolitan dailies, although their
news dispatches anticipate the special interests of the
public to whom they are addressed.

A correspondent for the *Afro-American* was one of
the three roving reporters in the news recently after
having entered Communist China for a first hand report
on that nation, but without authorization from the
State Department.

CHAPTER V

COMMERCIAL ASPECT OF THE NEGRO PRESS

A. THE NEWSPAPER AS A BUSINESS

Although newspapers may crusade for various causes, and take sides in factional disputes, it should be remembered that, in the words of the late William Allen White, the newspaper business is after all "just a business." This truism is equally applicable to the Negro press. Negro publishers and editors are first of all business men with a commodity for sale — the news. Their primary motivation is not uplift, but profit, although they seem to have found it to their advantage to combine the two. Limited as they are to the Negro market for their support, it has resulted in their exploiting to the fullest techniques that serve to gain the support of this market. This accounts in no small measure for the militancy which characterizes the papers with the larger circulations, and for the news emphasis discussed in the preceding chapter.

While there are some marginal enterprises, many of the smaller newspapers and those with the national circulations are substantial businesses. Forty of these publishing concerns are incorporated under the laws of the states in which they are published.[1] Capital investment in individual plants among the larger papers, ranges from $50,000 to more than a half mil-

---

[1] Bureau of the Census. *Negro Newspapers and Periodicals in the United States.* Washington, D.C.: Government Printing Office, Bulletin No. 1 (1945), p. 3.

lion dollars. In this latter case this would be, according to Bird and Merwin, the capital investment generally needed to publish a daily newspaper in a modern American city somewhat in excess of 50,000 population.[2]

All of the large newspapers and many of those in the middle size bracket, are equipped with modern rotary presses. The number of employees ranges from a few, in the case of the small individually operated newspapers to more than two-hundred.[3] This expansion in the number of employees, and the growth of increasingly impersonal relationships, has been accompanied by the seemingly inevitable strained relations between employees and employers. While the latter roundly denounced the policies of some unions for refusing to accept Negroes, these same newspapers frown on their own employees joining their respective unions. Staff members of more than a half dozen major newspapers have joined the *American Newspaper Guild.* At least two major strikes have occurred, tying up the publication of two newspapers with the larger circulations. In the case of the *Amsterdam News,* after eleven weeks of suspended publication, the owners were forced into bankruptcy and sold out. Local white *Guild* members, led by the late Heywood Broun, took a prominent part in the strike and helped out on the picket lines. The new owners readily came to an agreement with the *Guild,* and the newspaper resumed publication.

Eleven years ago some *Chicago Defender* employees went on strike when the Chicago Local of the *International Typographical Union* struck for a base pay of

---

[2] Bird and Merwin, *op. cit.,* p. 69.
[3] Bureau of Census: *op. cit.,* p. 3.

$100 a week. Although the *Defender* never suspended publication entirely, the strike lasted for several weeks until an agreement was reached.

Editorial comment regarding these strikes from some newspapers not involved, was not unlike that which any metropolitan sister paper would be likely to make under similar circumstances. One sees the identity of interests behind such phrases as "professional unionists," "international unionism," "defy and vitiate the Taft-Hartley law," "defies and nullifies," "a foolish and suicidal gesture," etc., while denouncing the "closed shop."

That some of these publications represent well established business enterprises is attested by the age of these journals. The median number of years of publication for the five newspapers on which this study is principally based, is fifty-four years.[4] The mean is also fifty-four years. Many other newspapers have long records of continuous publication. The *California Eagle* of Los Angeles began publication in 1879; the *Colorado Statesman* of Denver, 1890; the *Bulletin,* Tampa, Fla., 1914; the *Iowa Bystander* of Des Moines, 1894; the *Plain Dealer* of Kansas City, Kansas, 1899; the *Guardian*[5] of Boston, 1901. The Detroit *Tribune,* in the 25,000 - 30,000 circulation bracket, is not as old as those previously mentioned, having begun publication in 1922. The St. Louis *Argus* was first published in 1912; the *Kansas City Call,* 1919; the *Carolina*

---

[4] The *Pittsburgh Courier, Afro-American, Chicago Defender, Journal and Guide,* and the New York *Amsterdam News.*

[5] Under the editorship of William Monroe Trotter, the *Guardian* was once the most influential Negro newspaper in America. Around the turn of the century and shortly thereafter, it was a leader in the fight against the Booker T. Washington school of thought. It no longer has a national circulation.

Times, Durham, N. C., 1919; the *Cleveland Call and Post,* 1921; the *Houston Informer,* 1893; the *Northwest Enterprise* of Milwaukee, 1916; to mention a few.[6]

The ABC audited circulation ranges as high as 40,000 among these papers just cited. Several of the editors and publishers of these newspapers are highly respected in journalistic circles. Roscoe Dungee, editor of the *Black Dispatch,* is probably the most highly regarded editorial writer in the Negro press today.

While no figure would be entirely accurate in these times of uncertain monetary values, yet Oak's estimate of the total value of plants and equipment of all Negro owned publications at $10,000,000, is probably the most reliable figure available.[7]

Number and Circulation: During the year 1948, the base year of this study of political content (See Chapter II Methodology), secular Negro newspapers were being published in thirty-six states and the District of Columbia.[8] Four of those states without a Negro newspaper were in the New England region, and seven were in the west and northwest, all with a sparse Negro population.

There is no single authentic source of information regarding the number and circulation of these newspapers. Some new ventures have ceased publication by the time they have been listed by a recognized agency, thus making a list obsolete before it gets into general use.

A survey made by the United States Department of Commerce[9] in 1945, listed 155 Negro newspapers in

---

[6] Ayer and Son, *op. cit.*

[7] Oak, V.V. *The Negro Newspaper.* Yellow Springs, Ohio: Antioch College Press, 1948, p. 72.

[8] Oak, *op. cit.,* p. 66.

[9] Bureau of the Census: *op. cit.,* p. 1.

the United States at that time. However, *The Negro Handbook*, published in 1949, and based chiefly on 1948 data, lists 183 Negro-owned newspapers, and ninety-eight magazines and bulletins, compiled, so it says, "from various sources."[10] Oak, listed only 169 secular newspapers, but gave a total of over 325 periodicals of all types, including campus publications, religious, fraternal, general, bulletins and magazines.[11] The regional distributions of newspapers in the latter list were eighty-five published in the South, sixty-six in the North, and eighteen in the West. The northern papers constituted nearly 60 percent of an estimated total circulation of over two million. This is due chiefly to the national coverage of the big northern newspapers, and possibly to a higher rate of literacy and a predominantly urban population among northern Negroes. With one or two exceptions, the western and southern papers have only regional circulations.

The vast majority of the Negro newspapers are published weekly. Five are published semi-weekly, and three are dailies.[12] Several of the larger weeklies publish two or more editions, including a city, and a national edition. The *Pittsburgh Courier* leads in this department with fifteen editions — city, state or regional, and a national edition. This newspaper also leads in weekly circulation at 296,674, the largest in the history of the Negro press.[13]

The *Afro-American* group has the second largest circulation with approximately two hundred thousand

[10] Murray, Florence, (ed.) New York: The Macmillan Co., 1949, p. 310.

[11] Oak, *op. cit.*, p. 68.

[12] Murray, *op. cit.*, p. 310.

[13] N.W. Ayer and Sons' *Directory of Newspapers and Periodicals*, Philadelphia, Pa., 1949.

(199,926), published in seven different editions.[14] The home office in Baltimore publishes the national and two city editions, one of the latter appearing on Tuesday, and the other on Saturday. The remaining are the Washington, Philadelphia, Newark, and Richmond, Virginia editions.[15]

The *Chicago Defender* with a circulation of 189,-134,[16] publishes six editions under the name of that newspaper, and two subsidiaries whose circulations are not included in that figure.[17] The six editions of the *Defender* are: city — a daily tabloid, national, the southern, western, St. Louis, and Gary, Indiana.

The *Amsterdam News*, of New York City, with 83,143 in circulation, and *Norfolk Journal and Guide* at a 63,000 figure, round out the group of five large newspapers on which this study is based. The *News* is published in two editions — city and national — and the *Guide* publishes three: the national, the Peninsula, and home editions. All of these circulation figures are audited by the Audit Bureau of Circulation.

Four other newspapers with an ABC audit had circulations of approximately 25,000 or more. They were the Kansas City (Mo.) *Call*, the Cleveland *Call and Post*, Detroit *Chronicle*, and the Houston *Informer*. In all, twenty-two Negro newspapers were audited by ABC, with a combined circulation of over a million

---

[14] *Ibid,* compiled by totaling figures of various *Afro* newspapers, and Baltimore editions, as listed in this directory.

[15] The Washington, Philadelphia, Newark and Richmond *Afro-American* publications are given separate audits by ABC, and are listed in N.W. Ayer and Son's *Directory* as independent newspapers. In this study they are considered to be separate editions of the same newspaper, since they are printed in the home plant, and bear the same name.

[16] Ayer and Son, *op. cit.*

[17] Statement from *Chicago Defender* to writer.

copies, constituting approximately 50 percent of an estimated total circulation somewhat in excess of two million.[18]

The term "estimated" is used advisedly since other circulation figures are somewhat variable, being based on Post Office Statements, Sworn Statements, Publishers' Statements, and estimates of research students. It is of some significance to know, however, that during the ten-year period prior to 1948, the Negro newspapers approximately doubled their circulation. A growing interest in domestic and foreign, social and political issues brought on by the war, together with more favorable economic circumstances, were no doubt responsible for this rapid growth in circulation.

Chains. During the last two decades a number of consolidations among some newspapers, and expansions in the case of others, have resulted in the establishment of a few newspaper chains. The Scott Newspaper Syndicate is the largest of these chains in terms of the number of affiliated newspapers. This group of twelve newspapers is built around the Atlanta *Daily World*, first founded by W. A. Scott in 1928, as the Atlanta *World*, and established as a daily in 1932. Two semi-weeklies the Memphis *World* and Birmingham *World*, together with the other nine weeklies make up this newspaper chain. All but a few of the cooperating papers are located in southern cities. They have a combined circulation of (70,000).[19]

The Scott Syndicate functions also as a news agency. The Atlanta *World* in 1931 started the first rotogravure section published weekly by Negroes. This rotogravure syndicated section is now supplied to all member news-

---

[18] Ayer and Son, *op. cit.*, compilation of newspaper audits.

[19] Oak, *op. cit.*, p. 86.

papers, along with news, feature material, and editorials if so desired. Member newspapers send in to the home office local and regional news for syndicated distribution. The Atlanta *World* prints both a national and city edition. This chain also receives news service from the Associated Negro Press, International News Service as well as releases from the N.A.A.C.P. News Service.

The Scott newspapers have had considerable political influence in some southern cities in getting out the Negro vote in recent years. The Atlanta *World* in particular has crusaded consistently for political participation of Negro citizens in the city, state and nation.

Another chain of newspapers, the Houston *Informer* group, has grown up in Texas. There are four newspapers in this chain with a total ABC audited circulation of more than 46,000. The New Orleans *Informer and Sentinel* is the only paper in this group published outside of the state of Texas. The *Informer*, the largest in this chain with a circulation of over 27,000 began publication in 1893. This newspaper has had a stormy career as a militant advocate of Negro civic rights. It has lost its advertising on three occasions, and has been the victim of vandalism on the part of hostile whites.[20] It has stuck by its guns, and has a record of achievement in obtaining civic improvements such as better school facilities and teachers, better streets, and the addition of Negroes to the police force.

The *Afro-American Company* in addition to the Baltimore home office, maintains offices in Washington, D. C., Philadelphia, Newark, and Richmond. Each

---

[20] Detweiler, F.G., "The Negro Press Today." Amer. Jr. Soc., XLIV (1938), pp. 391-401.

of these publications is audited separately, and has its own editor. In various directories they are listed as individual newspapers.[21] It is in this sense that they may be considered as a chain. The Baltimore *Afro-American* was founded in 1891. It was purchased by John Henry Murphy in 1896, and has remained in the Murphy family since that time. The *Afro*-publications have the second largest circulation in the Negro press.[22]

The *Chicago Defender* has two affiliated subsidiaries, the Louisville (Ky.) *Defender,* and the *Michigan Chronicle* of Detroit. The latter two newspapers have a total ABC audited circulation of almost 42,000. The circulation of the *Defender* was more than 189,000. This publication has been probably the most controversial newspaper in the history of Negro journalism. Founded by the late Robert S. Abbott in 1905, it has consistently waged an uncompromising fight against any and all forms of American race discrimination and prejudice. Its militant policy has been denounced throughout the South and it was once banned by city ordinance in one Southern city, while a shipment of papers was burned in another.[23] It has been very popular among Southern Negroes, however, due chiefly to its vigorous campaign against the racial policies of that region. Today its national edition is approximately twice that of the home edition in circulation. Under the editorship of John H. Sengstache, it has not digressed materially from the militant course charted by its late founder.

Of late years, new ventures in the magazine field —

----

[21] Ayer and Son, *op. cit.;* Bureau of the Census, *op. cit.*

[22] In this study circulation figures of those publications have been totaled.

[23]Detweiler, F.G., *The Negro Press in the United States.* Chicago: University of Chicago Press, 1922, p. 157.

an area heretofore known for its failures — give every indication of succeeding. While less militant than the newspapers, at least a half dozen of these publications appear to be going concerns. In one case the circulation is well over a quarter-million copies monthly. The success of these journals is undoubtedly tied up with the improvement in the economic condition of the Negro masses.

B. NEWS GATHERING AGENCIES

There were fourteen Negro-operated news gathering agencies servicing Negro newspapers in 1945, according to the U. S. Bureau of the Census.[24] However, in reading these newspapers, one seldom encounters any releases from the majority of them. Some deal only in specialized news such as sports, or theatrical news, or feature articles and comics. Only a few are news agencies in the fullest sense of the term, and are important in the news distribution function.

The Associated Negro Press founded in 1919, is the oldest and has the largest number of subscribing newspapers. During World War II, there were as many as 112 member newspapers, although there are somewhat fewer than that at the present time.[25] The headquarters of ANP is located in Chicago. This agency functions as a co-operative news gathering and distributing organization, and membership is open to any newspaper of "good standing" which agrees to abide by the rules of the Association. This includes paying a membership fee and agreeing to cover news happenings in

---

[24] *Negro Newspapers and Periodicals in the United States,* 1945, Bulletin No. 1, p. 1.

[25] The Associated Negro Press. "The Story of the News." Unpublished mimeograph copy sent to writer by ANP.

their territory for transmission to the central office in Chicago.

The greater part of the news, however, is gathered by the ANP's own staff. These reporters are located "in every center of considerable Negro population . . . (and) strategic areas where experience has taught us that news of vital importance, or great interest is apt to break."[26] This includes representatives of ANP in the major cities of America, in three European capitals, the Virgin Islands, Africa, the West Indies, and the Canal Zone.

Until recently the *Associated Negro Press* was without a serious competitor in the distribution of news to Negro newspapers. In 1940 a group of publishers met in Chicago and formed the *Negro Newspaper Publishers' Association.* When the United States entered World War II the news center shifted to Washington, D. C., through which all important national and international news was funneled. The *Association* set up a central *News Bureau* in that city in 1944, and finally in 1947, the *National Negro Press Association* was established as an independent functional agency and has grown rapidly as a news agency.

From the beginning the *Publishers' Association* has received the hearty endorsement of Negro newsmen. The news distribution function, however, met with opposition from some of the larger newspapers. They felt that it would be merely duplicating news coverage already supplied by their own Washington staff correspondents. In January, 1948, the NNPA distributed news to thirty-three newspapers with an estimated circulation in excess of 800,000.[27]

---

[26] *Ibid.*, p. 1.
[27] Oak, *op. cit.*, p. 107.

The *Negro Newspaper Publishers Association* has been instrumental in improving the news coverage for Negro newspapers by getting Negro correspondents accredited to the White House Press Conference, (1944) and admitted to the Congressional Press Galleries in 1947. Negro newsmen have also been accredited to accompany official Presidential tours. The *Associated Negro Press,* too, is now represented in the Capital press galleries. The organization and function of the Scott Newspaper Syndicate as a news distribution agency has previously been discussed. This syndicate is the largest and most important in the South.

C. ADVERTISING IN THE NEGRO NEWSPAPERS

Today advertising has come to be the main source of revenue for the average American newspaper, but from the beginning it has been a weakness in the business organization of the Negro newspapers. First of all, as weekly newspapers they are at a disadvantage in competition with the dailies for the advertisers' dollar. Moreover, they are addressed to, and circulated among, a minority section of the population, known to be comparatively weak in purchasing power. Under these conditions commercial enterprises have been reluctant to pay for advertising space in the Negro papers. Some business establishments have been known to withdraw advertising when some of these sheets crusaded too vigorously on issues that clashed with the advertisers' interests. While this control technique, to be sure, is not confined to use against the Negro papers, yet due to their marginality in advertising revenue, it has posed the problem of whether to conform and keep this limited source of revenue, or to maintain free speech and suffer the consequences.

There is no uniformity in the manner in which various Negro newspapers have answered this question.

The inability to obtain a substantial amount of the more desirable advertising has been responsible for these newspapers taking what they could get, much of which has been of dubious quality. One may find good luck charms, dream books, and loadstones with mystic powers, sharing the same pages with cosmetics, food markets, department store ads, popular brand cigarettes, and alcoholic beverages. Perhaps no one is more aware of this deficiency than the Negro publishers themselves, and they are inclined to be sensitive and apologetic about the matter.

In his criticism of advertising in the Negro newspapers Westbrook Pegler struck a very sensitive spot, and one that is a source of embarrassment to some Negro newspapermen themselves. Roy Wilkins, then an *Amsterdam News* columnist cited earlier, conceded this point in his column when he expressed the opinion:

Westbrook Pegler wrote one true item in his column on the Negro press April 28. That was his assertion that the Negro Press, with its advertisements of "Lucky Magnetic Stones" and "Good Luck Powder" and "Success Books," is doing a disservice to its readers and misrepresenting their intelligence to the world at large.

Most readers will agree that some of the advertisements carried in the Negro press should be barred from its columns. There was a time when many of the papers needed any kind of advertising to keep alive. That is not true today and it is especially not true of our larger papers like the *Courier*, the *Defender*, the *Star News (Amsterdam News)*, the *Afro-American*, the *Journal and Guide*, the *Call*, and others.

These papers are money makers and some of them are big money makers. Everyone familiar with the publishing business knows that with economical management a 24 page newspaper which retails for ten cents can make money on circulation alone . . . all these papers own their own buildings and complete, modern printing plants. They have large, well trained staffs.

The point is, they don't need the money they get — say $1,000 to $2,000 a year — from these dubious advertisements. They can make it easily without that revenue. There is the further fact that these ads may be cutting them off from bigger and better lineage since advertising agencies for high class products (seeking any excuse for not going in Negro papers) may judge their reader market by lucky ads.[28]

Of recent years, however, the picture has improved considerably according to reports from various editors and publishers. The intercession of commercial advertising agencies in behalf of the Negro newspapers, on a commission basis, has been helpful. Likewise, the ABC auditing service, of which many of these newspapers have availed themselves, has tended to improve their advertising business. Many potential customers were reluctant to take sworn statements on circulation, as the basis of advertising rates.

The publication of two, or more, editions including a city and national edition, has also favored advertising in the local edition. Much advertisement is not carried in the national editions, since local enterprises will not pay for space to advertise their goods and services beyond the metropolitan region. One would not get a complete picture of advertisement in the Negro newspapers today from observations based on a national edition.

Some newspapers have been prominent in campaigns to induce white business enterprises located in Negro neighborhoods to employ Negroes. The Chicago *Whip*, and the Washington *Tribune*, were pioneers in this movement two decades ago. "Don't Buy Where you Can't Work", was the popular campaign slogan. This approach was accompanied by picketing, and

---

[28] *Amsterdam Star News.* May 9, 1942.

putting a boycott on those stores refusing to employ Negro clerks. Since the volume of Negro trade was large enough to be important, many stores found it good business policy to comply, and employed colored clerks. Such campaigns are indirectly bids for advertising in the local Negro newspapers.

The editors of six newspapers in answer to a question concerning the percentage of revenue derived from advertising, contributed the following information. Four of the large newspapers answered 60, 25, 40, and 60 percent respectively; and two average sized newspapers answered 75, 75 percent. Significantly, both the smaller newspapers, with larger proportionate local circulations, gave the highest and identical percentages of revenue derived from advertising. The median figure of 60 percent is not far below the national norm for dailies, which ranges from two-thirds to five-sixths of the total income.[29] The writer does not claim for these figures representativeness, however, since the sample is skewed in favor of the newspapers with big circulations, which constitute the universe for our primary interest — political content analysis. That the rank and file have not fared so well in getting the advertisers' dollar, is indicated by the findings of a Department of Commerce survey in 1945. While advertising lineage printed in some eighty Negro newspapers between July 1, 1944 and June 30, 1945 amounted to 2,967,230 inches, 74.5 percent of this volume of lineage went to fifteen newspapers.[30]

Failure to obtain substantial advertising has meant maximizing sales and sale price. The nationally cir-

---

[29] Bird and Merwin, *op. cit.*, p. 79.
[30] Bureau of Census, *op. cit.*, p. 2.

culated larger papers are now selling for fifteen and
twenty cents, having advanced their prices during the
war years from ten cents. It is doubtful if the large
newspapers could hold their circulation and keep this
price level if an economic slump were to occur.

Today, two or more Negro newspapers, and as many
magazines, are as likely to be found on news stands in
the downtown district, as in the predominantly Negro
neighborhoods. White news agencies handle them as
a matter of routine business. The colorful format of
some of them undoubtedly attracts the attention — and
less frequently the coins — of many white readers. Although one can only speculate on the extent to which
this occurs, it is general knowledge that public figures
keep well abreast of the currents of opinion in Negro
newspapers.[31] There is reason to believe that, at least
among the socially literate members of the white race,
what these journals say is becoming a matter of increas-
ing interest.

---

[31] An editorial on FEPC in the *Chicago Defender* (Feb. 28, 1948),
was entered, in full, in the *Congressional Record* (No. 38, March 1,
1948) by Senator Capper of Kansas.

Two Southern dailies, the *Nashville Banner* and *Birmingham News*,
asked, and were granted, permission to reprint George Schuyler's
Nov. 6, 1948 column "What's Good About the South."

Hodding Carter, a Mississippi editor, introduced excerpts from
Schuyler's column in radio forum, "America's Town Meeting of the
Air," Nov. 9, 1948.

CHAPTER VI

A NEW LOOK AT PROTEST

A. THE HISTORICAL SETTING

The socio-political history of the Negro in the United States has been that of an oppressed group, and it has been noted that the mark of oppression has found expression in his literary productivity. Robert T. Kerlin, a careful student of Negro life, made this observation more than a quarter-century ago, when he wrote:

> There is being produced in America a literature of which America, as the term is commonly understood, is not aware. It is a literature of protest — protest sometimes pathetic and prayerful, sometimes vehement and bitter. It comes from Negro writers, in prose and verse, in various forms of fiction, drama, essay, editorial and lyric.[1]

It is rather generally known that Negro newspapers likewise arose as organs of protest against certain undemocratic features of American society. And, as mentioned earlier, some students tend to characterize these journals today as being chiefly organs of protest, and think of the news function as being of lesser importance.

Burma, for example, says:

> That the present Negro press is first an organ of Negro protest and militancy and, second, a purveyor of Negro news, is both evident and admitted.[2]

---

[1] Kerlin, Robert T., *The Voice of the Negro.* New York: E.P. Dutton and Co., 1919, p. 229.

[2] Burma, *op. cit.,* p. 173.

There is little question regarding the militancy of a considerable section of the Negro press. Protest, too, is quite prominent in these journals. But, to the writer, the self-evident truth that protest is the primary function of the Negro newspapers today, needs a closer scrutiny.

When seen from an historical perspective the development of the Negro press falls easily into four well defined periods: the pre-Civil War period, and the post-Civil War period, the pre-World War period and the post-World War period. While there are no absolute lines of demarcation between these periods, and considerable overlapping is to be found, yet each is sufficiently individualized as to possess some characteristics of its own. This overview takes on added significance when, as in the present case, some students would tend to interpret the function of the Negro newspaper today, in terms of impressions based on its role in earlier historical settings.

The early Negro papers of the pre-Civil War period, were distinctly organs of propaganda and directed all of their efforts to the support of the abolition movement. The names of some of these early papers such as *Freedom's Journal, Rights for All, The Elevator, The Genius of Freedom,* and *The Liberator,* are suggestive of their anti-slavery policies. Available records show that *Freedom's Journal* was the first of these newspapers to appear, in the year 1827.[3] From that time until the Civil War there were sporadic appearances of so called newspapers — about twenty-six in all.[4] The name of Frederick Douglass is best known among these

---

[3] Detweiler, F.G., *The Negro Press in the United States.* Chicago: University of Chicago Press, 1922, p. 35.

[4] *The Negro Year Book.* 1921-22, p. 158.

early editors. His newspaper, *The North Star,* was re-
named *Frederick Douglass' Paper,* in order, he said, to
distinguish it from various other papers with "Stars"
in their titles.[5]

In the Post-Civil War period, the work of the abolition papers having been accomplished, they passed
from the scene and were followed by religious and de-
nominational organs which devoted much space to
problems of reconstruction, citizenship, and religion.
The *Christian Recorder* was first published before the
Civil War began, to be followed during the post-war
years, by the *Southwestern Christian Advocate,* the
American *Baptist,* the *Star of Zion,* the *Afro-Presby-
terian* and others of a similar nature. The financial
support afforded these periodicals by the denomina-
tional and fraternal bodies sponsoring them insured
them more security and greater longevity than had
been enjoyed by those of the pre-war period.

During this period there were also many editorial
sheets being published which could hardly be termed
newspapers. The late Mr. T. T. Fortune, former editor
of the *New York Age,* speaks of them as pamphlets.
He states: "For many years before and after 1880, until
our newspapers became established as vehicles of race
news, hopes and aspirations, thinkers of the race found
an outlet for their pent-up Utica in pamphlets. I had
a collection of some ten thousand or more of these
pamphlets when I disposed of my newspaper property
in 1907."[6]

It was not, however, until near the close of the
century that the Negro newspaper as we know it today,

---

[5] Detweiler, F.G., *op. cit.,* p. 41.
[6] *Ibid,* pp. 46-47.

emerged and was able to establish itself. Mr. L. M. Hershaw says of them in an article on the Negro press in 1906: "There are twenty-five or thirty (Newspapers) published by Negroes in different sections of the country which are really a credit to the profession of journalism."[7]

He divides the Negro newspapers of this time into four classes: school papers, religious papers, fraternal and beneficial papers, and secular newspapers to which belongs the great body of newspapers. Of this latter group, even at this early period, we find Negro editors divided on policies affecting Negro life. One group headed by the *Guardian* of Boston, whose editor was William Monroe Trotter, a graduate of Harvard University, claimed for the Negro all the natural, civil and political rights which inhere in man as man. This paper's motto was: "For Every Right with All Thy Might." It insisted upon the enjoyment of those rights now, without restrictions and reservations not applicable to other men. The other group of editors led by T. T. Fortune, of the *New York Age,* preached the postponement, for the present, of civil and political rights for the Negro, for economic and educational development, and emphasized industrial education.

Each of these two opposing camps found support in the leading Negro newspapermen of the day. William Calvin Chase, editor of the *Washington Bee,* H. C. Smith, of the *Cleveland Gazette, The Conservation* of Chicago and *The Advance* of St. Louis, were among the more militant group. The *Tribune* of Philadelphia, edited by Chris J. Perry, *The Independent,* of Atlanta, *The Planet,* of Richmond, *The Freeman* of Indianapolis, whose editor was George Knox, and John H.

---

[7] Hershaw, L.M., "The Negro Press." Charities, XV (1905), p. 68.

Murphy's *Afro-American Ledger,* of Baltimore, headed up the conservative element. The points of view held by the opposing groups of journalists were not fundamentally different from the two schools of thought made famous by two of the most outstanding American Negroes, W. E. B. DuBois and Booker T. Washington.

The new tone of militancy which was again developing in Negro journalism around the turn of the century, may be traced to contemporary maladjustments which had appeared in race relations, chiefly in the South. Certain legislation known as the Black Codes, passed by many Southern states, had taken away the Negroes' newly acquired rights of citizenship, and had seriously hampered his economic opportunities. The withdrawal of Federal troops from the South, by order of President Hayes, removed what protection the freedmen had enjoyed. Thereafter, they were intimidated and kept away from the polls while legislation was passed which took away from them the ballot. The Ku Klux Klan and the Night Riders were persecuting Negroes, and lynchings during the ten year period, 1890-1900, reached an all time high mark.[8]

Finally a number of race riots of serious proportions occurred in Atlanta, in Springfield, Illinois, and New York City, all of which stimulated the birth of the National Association for the Advancement of Colored People, in 1910. DuBois came to New York City from Atlanta University to become its Director of Publicity and Research, and editor of *The Crisis,* its official organ.

Militant Negro journalism of the pre-World War I period, received its greatest impetus from the pen of W. E. B. DuBois. Other Negro university graduates

---

[8] *Negro Year Book,* 1918-1919, p. 375.

who were contributors to periodicals of this time, Kelley Miller, William Monroe Trotter, and J. W. E. Bowen, were also critical of the conservatism and influence of the great leader, Booker T. Washington. While they recognized his ability and paid due tribute to his achievements, yet they differed with his social philosophy, and protested against the legal discriminations and injustices being imposed upon the Negro in the South. DuBois very clearly sets forth their points of disagreement:[9]

"Mr. Washington represents in Negro thought the old attitude of adjustment and submission . . . (he) distinctly asks that black people give up, at least for the present, three things — First, political power; Second, insistence on civil rights; Third, higher education of Negro youth — and concentrate all their energies on industrial education, the accumulation of wealth and the reconciliation of the South. This policy has been courageously and insistently advocated for over fifteen years, and has been triumphant for perhaps ten years. As a result of this tender of the palm branch, what has been the return? In these years have occurred:

1. The disfranchisement of the Negro.
2. The legal creation of a distinct status of civil inferiority for the Negro.
3. The steady withdrawal of aid from institutions for the higher training of the Negro.

These movements are not, to be sure, direct results of Mr. Washington's teachings; but his propaganda has, without a shadow of a doubt, helped their speedier accomplishment. Is it possible and probable that nine million men can make effective progress in economic lines if they are deprived of political rights, made a servile caste, and allowed only the most meager chances of developing their exceptional men?"

The death of Booker T. Washington, shortly after the organization of the N.A.A.C.P., removed whatever influence he may have had in stemming the current

---

[9] DuBois, W.E.B., *The Souls of Black Folk*. Chicago: A.C. McClurg 1920 (12th edit.), p. 50.

of growing militancy in Negro journalism led by *The Crisis* magazine. This militancy gathered momentum during World War I, and has continued to the present time in the leading Negro newspapers.

It may be seen from the foregoing that social reform was the motivating force that brought the Negro newspapers into existence. They were established primarily as journals of anti-slavery opinion. The reform note and protest continue to be the dominant themes in editorial opinion. Few people today, however, buy newspapers primarily to read the editorial or opinion section — not even the Negro newspapers. It is this change in the function of the Negro newspapers that many students have failed to take into account. Kerlin had noted the growing importance of the news function in these papers when he wrote:

> The colored people in America are going to their own papers in these days for the news and for their guidance in thinking. . . Wherever in all the land there is a considerable Negro population, there is a Negro newspaper.[10]

Detweiler, too, called attention to this development in his more recent article, "The Negro Press Today", in which he said:

> The Negro paper began as an extended editorial, but has been gradually justifying itself as a newspaper. More and more it is becoming necessary to its people as a purveyor of news.[11]

A more literate and articulate Negro reading public is turning to its own newspapers for their news value, to see what Negroes are doing and what is being done to them. In this connection the Negro newspapers

---

[10] Kerlin, *op. cit.*, Introduction.

[11] Detweiler, F.G., "The Negro Press Today." *American Journal of Sociology*, XLIV, No. 3 (November, 1938), p. 399.

perform a special service for their readers which the white dailies do not perform. Protest may be apparent in some news articles where it would seem that Negroes are adversely affected by the social situation to a greater extent than other elements in the population. But it is the news value of the incident that attracts the attention of the Negro readers, although protest may be present.

B. THE QUANTITATIVE APPROACH

The application of quantitative techniques to test the hypothesis that the Negro papers are primarily organs of protest, has likewise failed to sustain this view. Social reform also has its constructive aspect. The reformer offers a remedial program of action, which, it is alleged, will correct or improve a condition held by him to be undesirable. Although negativism, the objective index to protest, is present, we should exercise considerable caution in assuming that protest is the dominant factor in reader appeal. The larger percentage of positive scores would seem to indicate that these newspapers stand "for" something, as well as register opposition to some aspects of our cultural life. In these newspapers, from a quantitative point of view, protest as manifested by negative scores, takes second place to the advocacy of positive values consistent with the ideal patterning of American culture. (See Table VII) The editorial section, for example, where basic policy is elaborated, shows more than 60 percent positive or constructive scores, as compared with less than 35 percent negative symbols. This latter figure represents a significant enough amount of negativism to provide a plausible basis for identifying these newspapers as primarily journals of protest. But this is an impressionistic conclusion, rather than a demonstrable one. It is a conclusion based on a one sided focus on the content of these papers; one that fails to take into account the greater emphasis placed on the promotion of fundamental values and aspirations historically characteristic of American society. (See Table XVI)

CHAPTER VII

SUMMARY AND CONCLUSIONS

It may now be helpful to bring together some of the more significant inferences which may be derived from the statistical data presented in this study, and to make a mental note of possible broader implications which would seem to be tenable.

1. The central hypothesis that was being tested — namely that the Negro newspapers reflect those values consistent with the "American Tradition," rather than the espousal of doctrines alien to it — was sustained.

2. The fundamental concern of the political comment in these Negro papers is with the promotion of civil liberties and other citizenship rights for the whole population.

3. There is uncompromising rejection of the social practices affecting adversely the status and role of colored minorities in American society. Segregation and discrimination lead the list of such rejected practices.

4. The relatively infrequent use of communist symbols eliminates this focus as a point of major emphasis in these Negro papers. The attitudes expressed toward these symbols when used were almost entirely unfavorable.

5. The tendency on the part of some students to characterize the Negro newspapers as primarily organs of protest, was not sustained in this study. We would

be more justified in regarding them as journals of reform, since it is demonstrated statistically that the major emphasis of these papers is with the promotion of positive values which are held to be desirable. Although protest is prominent, it is essentially a constructive press, and is undoubtedly a valuable agency in the molding of public opinion.

6. The percentage of foreign news in the Negro papers studied is about the same as that of the Metropolitan dailies.

7. Editorial comment is very favorable to the American people, and to American ideals, but registers sharp disapproval of America as a social system.

8. Great faith was manifested in the Constitution of the United States, and in the Supreme Court, both of which were viewed as instruments favorable to the achievement of the aspirations of minorities.

9. The South, as a region, Southerners, the Southern wing of the Democratic Party, and all Southern political symbols, find in the Negro papers a decidedly negative response. There is nothing in their expressed attitudes that would indicate agreement with the Southern white man's declared position that he is the Negro's best friend.

10. The North is given more favorable comment, but even so, there is considerable editorial criticism of its failure to accept colored minorities as equals in many areas of social life.

11. Significantly, President Truman was given more favorable than unfavorable editorial comment, in this a predominantly Republican press. The Democratic Party, too, was accorded a favorable reception, although not to the same extent as that of the titular head of the party.

12. Among the top Republicans, Governor Dewey was by far the favorite personality in editorial opinion. He received a larger ratio of favorable to unfavorable comment than did President Truman. Governor Dewey's alleged liberal record on civil rights legislation in the state of New York was usually cited.

13. While four of the five newspapers comprising our universe supported the Republican Party in 1948, editorial comment was decidedly unfavorable to the 80th Congress, the controversial Republican dominated congress.

14. Henry Wallace's Progressive Party was rejected without exception in the editorials, but Mr. Wallace, himself, was accorded favorable reception.

15. World organization, as represented by the United Nations organization, was given unanimous support as a means of stabilizing international relations.

16. Warfare was rejected overwhelmingly as an instrument for the settlement of international problems, even though it was recognized that racial minorities have in the past made significant gains as the result of wars.

17. There was some variation among these newspapers with regard to points of emphasis in news and comment, yet one fundamental fact brought out in this study was the homogeneity in the statistical categories. This generalization is in marked contrast with the findings of M. M. Willey in his study, *The Country Newspaper,* in the New England region, where he found "unduly wide variation" among the categories.

While in the thinking of many publicists and professional patriots, any criticism of America, or its institutions is considered to be the psychological equivalent of disloyalty, or subversive activity, it should not be overlooked that the climate of opinion is an important variable in the definition of the act. It goes without saying that criticism, and reform, have historically been part and parcel of the American story. They are not in themselves alien to the American dream, but have been oriented toward its realization. Social reform and the idea of progress are complementary, and social reformers have played a significant role in the realization of the idea.

The Negro newspapers are waging an all-out effort against second-class citizenship for racial minorities in American society. They unanimously endorse the efforts of the National Association for the Advancement of Colored People in this respect. They are firm believers in the Federal Courts, and in the Constitution. It is inconceivable to the Negro editor that he should be considered as un-American and/or subversive for working for the extension of democratic liberties within the framework of the Constitutional system. Rather, he considers as un-American those who would withhold such liberties from other citizens.

The presence of a considerable amount of protest in the Negro papers has been misinterpreted by many of their critics. This is quite a normal development in American journalism, and is a manifestation of the historic crusading spirit. In a minority press this emphasis is probably a function of the degree of integration and security, or the lack of it, enjoyed by the reading public to whom it is addressed. It is a fact that the more aggressive among these papers are those with the larger circulations, although it may prove difficult to establish a causal relationship, because of the presence of numerous other factors which enter into the situation.

Another aspect of the Negro newspapers that is generally overlooked, or ignored, is their basic conservatism on matters other than racial democracy. The Negro in American society is subject to the same controls and pressures which are in operation on the general population. He speaks the same language, professes the same religion, wears the same clothing and eats the same foods. The cultural heritage of the African has long since disappeared, or has been modified beyond recognition. Thus, as this culture imposes itself upon the American Negro there is no culture clash, no resistance offered to it. Unlike the Immigrant Press, which is addressed to a minority with an unbroken cultural tradition, the Negro newspapers reflect an unquestioned acceptance of the prevailing middle-class mores and values. Their criticism is directed against barriers that tend to restrict the Negro's participation in the social order, rather than against the nature of the social order itself.

Many symbols of middle-class conformity are quite prominent in the Negro papers. Such features as reviews of current literature, and art, bridge chats, and magazine sections, all have their publics. There is a great deal of emphasis given to society news, as mentioned earlier. It is in this realm of social life, that these newspapers reflect the extent to which Negro culture seeks to conform to majority group values. Standards of beauty are definitely white standards. Women pictured are almost invariably very light in color with thin features. A prominent place is given to the well tailored "socialites" — smiling men and women of the professional and business class — who are carriers of the middle class success symbols, and middle class mores.

It should also be recalled that four of the five newspapers studied here, although self-styled as independent, were staunch supporters of the Republican Party in the Presidential election of 1948. Only one of these four newspapers was published south of the Potomac River. The fifth, a supporter of the Democratic Party was anything but politically radical. It dropped one of its best columnists, a white journalist, for his persistent Progressive Party leanings during the 1948 campaign. During the course of the 1952 Presidential election, one of the Republican journals fired its highly regarded city editor, apparently for lack of enthusiasm for that journal's editorial policy. These are not exceptional cases, but involve men of higher caliber than usual. Many working journalists are let out from time to time for reasons other than competence, while others complain about restrictions imposed in the handling of local material. The Negro journalist on the big papers is probably as subject to the pressures stemming from editorial policy, as is his counterpart on the white metropolitan dailies.

While there can be little question but that the Negro newspapers play a significant role in providing raw material out of which public opinion is molded in the Negro community, it is not so easy to ascertain the real influence they have in shaping political opinion. Other mass media of communications, the daily newspapers and magazines, radio and television, likewise play an important part in that process. Negro editors, like the white, are often caught up in party politics, or factional rivalry so that opposing political views may be espoused by different Negro journals in the same city. Four of the five leading newspapers, however, were without serious competition in the metropolitan area.

In 1948 four of this same group supported the winning party in their respective states. In 1952 three of them were on the winning side. These newspapers, however, showed a greater attachment to the Republican Party than did the Negro voters. In 1948, the preponderantly Democratic Negro vote was generally considered to have been the decisive margin of victory. But in the recent presidential elections the Negro vote was less important.

Another development of some significance has been the recent trend toward lowering the racial barriers in journalism. Various white writers who have been contributors to the Negro journals have given them something of an inter-racial flavor. Two white journalists are employed as editors of major publications.

Perhaps of greater significance has been the employment of a number of Negro journalists on some of the white dailies. While in the past, several of the white papers engaged Negro writers to edit the "Negro News," today more than twenty of the dailies employ Negro reporters and writers who get general assignments. One of these, Carl T. Rowan, of the Minneapolis *Star Tribune,* is the author of the best seller, *South of Freedom.*

The editor of the Milwaukee *Journal* said recently of Bob Teague, writer on the sports staff: "Mr. Teague's being a Negro has nothing to do with our employing him. We told Teague whether he remained or not depended on his work. He has come up to expectations and made a place for himself."

All things considered the outlook for Negro journalism appears to be promising. In contrast with the European Immigrant Press, the Negro Press is unlikely to disappear in the predictable future. For while the immigrant is losing his identity as such and merging into the population, the Negro shows no likelihood of the loss of his racial identity.

There can be little doubt, however, but that the Negro newspapers that survive in the future must be prepared to meet a keener competition from other mass media of communications, including radio and television as well as the metropolitan dailies. There is a growing concern throughout the world with the aspirations of the masses of colored peoples of the underdeveloped areas, and with civil rights as the term pertains to the American Negro population. This interest was given impetus by the Supreme Court decision of 1954 removing the legal barriers to public school integration. A number of other court decisions and legislative enactments have likewise tended to establish the legal basis for a wider participation of the Negro in the economic, political and social life of the nation. The news interest stemming from the conflicts and compromises which these changes have engendered, news which in the past has been the life blood of the Negro press, is becoming a commonplace on the front pages of the daily press and is being headlined in newspapers around the world. The Negro people no longer need wait for the appearance of their favorite weekly for a perusal of current events along the racial frontier, particularly where the big news stories are concerned.

The Negro publishers are already feeling the effects of this competition. There has been a significant decrease in circulation among these publications during the last decade. Although it is not clear the extent to which this loss in circulation is related to an increase in the price of these journals, there is little doubt but that the invasion of their special news domain by the white dailies has been a major factor in this development. One of the leading Negro newspapers, the *Chicago Defender,* has responded to this new challenge by publishing its own daily, a tabloid edition of more general news interest, as well as the weekly national edition. The tabloid edition carries an I.N.S. summary of world news, Columnists Robert Spivack and Bennett Cerf, as well as other features common to all dailies. Various other Negro journals now publish bi-weekly editions. The *Atlanta World* has published a daily edition for many years.

There is still a place in American life for the Negro newspaper. The white dailies are devoted primarily to straight reporting of news of racial significance. Very often background material is too limited, or too impersonal to satisfy the special interest of this racial minority. It is this supplemental news function of the Negro papers that commends them to their readers. So long as there are divisive forces in operation in American society which tend to create problems of special concern to the Negro community, they will continue to turn to their own journals to see what additional illumination they can bring to bear on the lingering shadows of racism.

APPENDIX I-A

POLITICALLY SIGNIFICANT SYMBOLS

Coding Procedure. Each symbol is scored in keeping with the manner in which it is presented in context. When presented favorably it is given a positive (+) score; when presented unfavorably it is given a negative (−) score. Other presentations are given a neutral (0) score.

Absolutism:

Authoritarianism:

America, (See United States):

Americans:
    American citizens, American people, all American, American citizenship.

American Tradition:
    American concepts of equality, American democracy, American democratic ideals, American dream, American heritage, American ideal, American ideals, American legacy, American principle, American principles, American story, American way, American way of life, heritage of the whole American people, high ideals of American citizenship, in American terms, the American promise our heritage, the democracy we profess, the spirit of America, the traditional American way, those fundamental principles, sense of fair play, fundamental American liberties.

Anarchy:

Appeasement:

Argentina:

Attlee, Clement:

Australia:

Belgium:

Britain, Great; (England)
    Britain, England, the Islands, the United Kingdom, English, Parliament, all nationals (except Churchill and Attlee), All cities (London etc.) coded as G.B., British.

British Empire:
> British colonies, Colonial rule, British rule, British crown, the British colonies, Colonial office.

Bolshevism:

Capitalism:
> Big business, big financial interests, capitalist, corporations, the group which controls and owns the production machinery of the country.

China:

China (Nationalist):

Churchill:

Civil Liberties (Rights):
> All rights, a fundamental right, a right of citizens, Bill of Rights, Civil Rights law 1866, civil rights, democratic rights, full rights, fundamental rights of citizenship, human rights, moral rights, our rights, rights under the constitution, rights as citizens, Negro rights, status as a citizen.

Chiang Kai Shek:

Collectivism:

Common good:
> advantage of all Americans, all American children, common interests, common well being, for the benefit of all its citizens, social security, for all people.

Common man:
> average United States citizen, common people, little people, the people, we the masses, the American citizen who has no personal advantage at stake in the election.

Communism:
> communist, communist party, Das Kapital, Marxist, reds, Marxism, Marxian theses, Marx the prophet.

Congress (80th):

Consent of the Governed:

Constitution (U.S.):
> (Amendments to, coded same), Fourteenth Amendment, constitutional rights, constitutional birth right, constitutional, constitutional law, constitutionality.

Conservative:

Democracy:
democratic, democratic ideals, democratic ideas, democratic institutions, democratic life, democratic policy, democratic principles, democratic process, democratic nation, democratic treatment, democratic society, democratic system, the democratic way, the democratic way of life, Republic, Republican form of government, democratic structure of society.

Democracies, the:

Democratic Party:
Democrats, Democratic National Committee, Democratic convention, Democratic primaries.

Democrats, Southern (see Southern Democrats):

Dewey:

Despotism:

Dictatorship:
dictator, totalitarianism, authoritarianism.

Disarmament:

Discrimination:
make shift, injustice, excluded because of race, discriminatory hiring practices, discriminatory, color discrimination, compelled to pay higher rents, employment bias, inferior facilities, job discrimination, inequality of treatment, excluded from membership, limited employment, practice of hiring Negroes only in the lower service brackets, refusing to serve, registration bias, racial quotas, restriction, restrictive covenants, second class citizenship, step citizenship, unequal, unequal facilities, replaced (colored workers) with unemployed white (workers), white primary, for white only, inequity.

Dixiecrats:
States righters, States Rights Party, Dixie diehards, the stop Truman democrats, the rebellious Democrats.

Dutch, the:

Empire:

Equality:
admitted to graduate and professional schools, all Americans the same, all persons regardless of race, creed or color; common

level, equal, equitable, equal education, equal rights, equal break, equal facilities, equal educational facilities, equal treatment, equalized facilities, equal opportunity, equal vote, equal services, equal salaries, equal job opportunity, equal recreational facilities, equally as much as, equal teacher pay, equalization, first class Americans, first class citizenship, full fledged citizenship, full membership, full participation, full citizenship, free of jim crow, integration, one class of citizenship, open to all comers, on equal terms, on the same footing, no distinction, non segregated, political equality, single standards of treatment for all, single standards of citizenship, substantially equivalent, substantial equality, treated as American citizens, unsegregated, without distinction, without regard to race, true citizenship, social equality.

England, (coded Great Britain):

Ethiopia:
Abbysenia, Haile Selassie.

Fascism:
fascist, gestapo like.

F. E. P. C.:
Fair employment bill, Ives-Fulton bill.

F. B. I.:

France:
French, all nationals, all cities (Paris etc.) coded as France.

Franco:

Freedom:
as free men, free, free state, free government, free speech, free forever, free from illegal restraint, economic freedom, to be free, to set free.

Free enterprise:
free competition, individual initiative, private enterprise.

Franchise:
at the polls, enfranchise, enfranchisement, ballot rights, free vote, popular vote, suffrage, the ballot, the right to vote, to participate freely in the process of representative government, vote, voting, voters, the vote.

Germany:
German, all nationals (except Hitler), all cities.

Great Britain:

Greece:

Greek, Republicans:

Greek, Rebels:

Hitler:
    Der Führer, Mein Kampf.

Imperialism:
    colonialism, colonial exploitation, exploiters, exploitation of natives, exploited colonial subjects, empire, imperialist, imperial crowd, the colonial system, under the white man's foot, stepping on colonial people.

Internationalism:
    global, international relation, (United Nations-coded separately), United States leadership in the world, the world, world commonwealth, world wide responsibilities.

Independence:
    independent.

Isolationism:
    isolationist.

Jews:
    Jewish, Judaism.

Justice:
    fair treatment, just due.

Labor Party:
    Labor Party, Labor Government, the British Socialist government.

Latin America:
    Any reference to Central, and South American countries, and their nationals.

Liberia:
    Any reference to Liberia, Monrovia, or nationals.

Liberty:
    liberation, liberated, political liberty.

Liberalism:
    liberal, liberals, liberalizing, liberal spirit, liberal tradition, liberal views, liberalizing opinion, a crusader.

Marshall Plan:
> European Recovery Program, The Truman Plan, the aid to Europe bill.

Militarism:
> war, warfare, warmonger, warmongering, call to arms, mass slaughter.

Mussolini:

N.A.A.C.P.:
> National Association for the Advancement of Colored People.

Nationalism:

Nazism:

Nationalization:

New Deal:
> New dealers.

North, the:
> northern cities, northerners, northern conservatives, northern elements, the northern states.

Oppressive Laws:
> Oppression, domination by law.

Peace:

Progressive Party:
> the new party, third party, Wallacites, Wallace group.

Privilege, special:

Poll tax:
> a fee for the right to exercise the franchise.

Racism:
> anti-semitism, aryans, a white empire, Bilboism, a mistake to try to lift colored people, color bias, master race, master race ideas, Negrophobia, racist, race hate, race egotism, race bigots, race bigotry, race bias, race hating, racial evils, race riots, race superiority propaganda, race baiting, race haters, race purity, crazy notions about race, Rankinism, the color line, white supremacy, white supremacists, white is right, won't allow colored persons into country, emphasis on whiteness, racial immorality, racial doctrine, racial intolerance, race poisoned, white primary.

Reform:
  crusaders, reformers.

Republican party:
  G.O.P., Republicans, Republican National Committee, Republican National convention, Republican Primaries.

Responsibility:

Representative Government:

Revolution:

Roosevelt:
  F.D.R.

Russia:
  behind the iron curtain, Kremlin, the Soviets, Russians, all nationals, all cities (Moscow etc.), coded as Russia Politbureau.

Segregation:
  caste, caste system, color caste, color bar, all white, exclude because of race or color, double (racial) standard, ghetto, jim crow, lily white, on a segregated basis, to bar colored, separate, segregationist, separate equality separate but equal, for white only, racially separate basis, would not serve colored, solely white, "gold and silver" standard in Panama, race segregation.

Slavery:
  bondage, enslave, enslavement, serf, serfdom, slave, slaves.

South Africa:

South America, (coded Latin America):

South, the:
  deep south, dixie, dixieland, below the Mason and Dixon line, South, the solid south, southern states, the southern region, (three or more states listed together), the southern scene, southern.

Southerners:
  dixieites, dixie Senators, dixie slave holders, dixie whites, dixie statesmen, southern delegates, southern Governors, southern whites, southern Senators, southern race haters, southern pecks, southern rebels, the Negro hating South, white southerners, young southern whites, white residents of the South, southern demagogues, white men from the deep South, the southern forces, (three or more persons from the South listed together), the southern block, white friends in the South, reactionary Bourbons.

Southern Democrats:
  Dixiecrats, dixie Democrats, southern Democratic primaries, southern white primary, Democratic primary in the South, (three or more southern Democrats listed together), rebel Democrats.

Socialism:
  socialists.

Stalin:
  the Russian dictator.

Supreme Court:
  highest court, the high court, United States Supreme Court.

Taft:

Taft-Hartley Bill:

Tito:

Truman:
  The President.

Tyranny:

T.V.A.:

United Nations:
  any branch of U.N.

United States (coded as America):
  America, Americana, Congress, the Federal Government, State Department, Civil Service Board, the Nation, the Government, Uncle Sam, (Supreme Court, coded separately).

Vatican:
  the Pope.

War:
  (coded militarism).

Wallace:
  the Third Party candidate, Progressive Party leaders.

Western Europe:

Welfare State:

Zionism:
  Israel, Jewish State, Palestine, State of Israel.

APPENDIX I-B

DERIVED SYMBOL LIST FOR TESTING BASIC HYPOTHESIS
Note. The original symbol list was submitted to a panel of eight
well known students of American cultural dynamics for scoring. If
considered to be consistent with the spirit of the American creed,
the symbol was given a (+) score, if contrary, a (−) score. Other
symbols considered to have no bearing on the creed, were given a
neutral (0) score. Agreement of seven of the eight panel members
on any symbol, was regarded as sufficient for its inclusion:

1. Absolutism
2. Anarchy
3. Bolshevism
4. Civil Liberties
5. Common Good
6. Common Man
7. Communism
8. Consent of Governed
9. Constitution, U.S.
10. Democracy
11. Despotism
12. Dictatorship
13. Discrimination
14. Equality
15. Fascism
16. F.E.P.C.
17. Franco
18. Freedom
19. Free Enterprise
20. Franchise
21. Hitler
22. Imperialism
23. Independence
24. Justice
25. Liberty
26. Liberalism
27. Militarism
28. Mussolini
29. Nazism
30. Oppressive Laws
31. Privilege Special
32. Poll Tax
33. Racism
34. Reform
35. Representative Government
36. Responsibility
37. Roosevelt
38. Segregation
39. Slavery
40. Stalin
41. Supreme Court
42. Tyranny

APPENDIX II TABLES

TABLE VIII. PERCENTAGE DISTRIBUTION OF POLITICALLY
SIGNIFICANT SYMBOLS BY PAPER AND NEWS AND OPINION

Paper	Total	News	Opinion
Courier	25.38	57.57	42.42
Afro-American	21.97	74.33	25.66
Journal & Guide	18.51	70.39	29.60
Amsterdam News	9.62	58.51	41.58
Defender	24.50	47.59	52.39
Total	99.98	61.26	38.73

TABLE IX. PERCENTAGE DISTRIBUTION OF POLITICALLY
SIGNIFICANT SYMBOLS BY NEWSPAPER AND SCORE

Paper	Total	Positive (+1)	Negative (−1)	Neutral (0)
Courier	25.38	37.35	40.22	22.03
Afro-American	21.97	42.58	33.21	24.21
Journal & Guide	18.51	44.64	31.14	24.20
Amsterdam News	9.62	40.67	34.04	25.28
Defender	24.50	41.87	37.95	20.17
Total	99.98	41.38	35.85	22.76

TABLE X. NUMBER OF POLITICALLY SIGNIFICANT
SYMBOLS BY PAPER AND SECTION

Paper	Number of Symbols			
	Total	News	Columns	Editorials
Courier	2,588	1,490	843	255
Afro-American	2,240	1,665	313	262
Journal & Guide	1,888	1,329	358	201
Amsterdam News	981	573	260	148
Defender	2,498	1,189	942	367
Total	10,195	6,246	2,716	1,233

TABLE XI. PERCENTAGE DISTRIBUTION OF POLITICALLY
SIGNIFICANT SYMBOLS BY PAPER AND SECTION

Paper	Total	News	Columns	Editorials
Courier	25.38	57.57	32.57	9.85
Afro-American	21.97	74.33	13.97	11.69
Journal & Guide	18.51	70.39	18.96	10.64
Amsterdam News	9.62	58.41	26.50	15.08
Defender	24.50	47.59	37.71	14.68
Total	99.98	61.26	26.64	12.09

TABLE XII. AVERAGE NUMBER OF POLITICALLY
SIGNIFICANT SYMBOLS
PER ARTICLE BY PAPER AND SECTION

Paper	Total	News	Columns	Editorials
Courier	5.55	4.41	9.03	6.70
Afro-American	3.85	3.55	5.69	4.51
Journal & Guide	3.89	3.37	6.55	5.59
Amsterdam News	4.21	3.20	7.87	7.05
Defender	4.13	3.13	5.70	6.10
Total	4.30	3.55	6.82	5.79

TABLE XIII. PERCENTAGE DISTRIBUTION OF
POLITICALLY SIGNIFICANT SYMBOLS
BY PAPER AND SCORE: COLUMNS

Paper	Total	Positive (+1)	Negative (−1)	Neutral (0)
Courier	31.03	32.50	44.96	22.52
Afro-American	11.52	35.14	36.74	28.11
Journal & Guide	13.18	45.53	32.96	21.50
Amsterdam News	9.58	36.92	40.00	23.07
Defender	34.68	35.78	38.85	24.30
Total	99.99	36.08	40.20	23.71

TABLE XIV. PERCENTAGE DISTRIBUTION OF
POLITICALLY SIGNIFICANT SYMBOLS
BY PAPER AND SCORE: EDITORIALS

Paper	Total	Positive (+1)	Negative (−1)	Neutral (0)
Courier	20.68	40.39	41.96	17.64
Afro-American	21.24	41.98	41.22	16.79
Journal & Guide	16.30	52.23	34.32	13.43
Amsterdam News	12.00	50.67	30.40	18.92
Defender	29.77	46.04	43.05	10.89
Total	99.99	45.58	39.49	14.92

TABLE XV. NUMBER OF SYMBOLS BY SECTION AND SCORE
SIGNIFICANT FOR AMERICAN CREED

Paper	Total	Positive (+1)	Negative (−1)	Neutral (0)
News	3,152	1,656	1,199	297
Editorials	640	390	222	28
Columns	1,217	635	467	115
Total	5,009	2,681	1,888	440

TABLE XVI. PERCENTAGE DISTRIBUTION OF SYMBOLS
BY SECTION AND SCORE
SIGNIFICANT FOR AMERICAN CREED

Paper	Total	Positive (+1)	Negative (−1)	Neutral (0)
News	62.92	52.53	38.03	9.42
Columns	24.29	52.18	38.37	9.44
Editorials	12.77	60.93	34.68	4.37
Total	99.98	53.52	37.69	8.78

TABLE XVII. PERCENTAGE DISTRIBUTION OF POLITICALLY
SIGNIFICANT SYMBOLS BY PAPER AND SCORE: NEWS

Paper	Total	Positive (+1)	Negative (−1)	Neutral (0)
Courier	23.85	42.85	33.23	23.90
Afro-American	26.65	44.08	31.29	24.62
Journal & Guide	21.28	43.26	30.17	26.56
Amsterdam News	9.17	39.79	32.28	20.09
Defender	19.03	45.41	34.81	19.76
Total	99.98	42.85	33.23	23.90

TABLE XVIII. DISTRIBUTION OF POLITICAL SYMBOLS
RELATING TO AMERICAN CREED
IN ORDER OF OCCURRENCE

SYMBOLS CONSISTENT WITH THE CREED		SYMBOLS OPPOSED TO THE CREED	
Symbol	Number of Scores	Symbol	Number of Scores
Civil Liberties	592	Segregation	636
Equality	465	Discrimination	561
Franchise	290	Racism	257
Democracy	286	Communism	183
Supreme Court	250	Poll Tax	110
Constitution	218	Hitler	56
Freedom	201	Slavery	51
F.E.P.C.	166	Imperialism	44
Justice	163	Fascism	34
Liberalism	143	Nazism	32
Roosevelt	71	Dictatorship	27
Liberty	58	Stalin	27
Independence	36	Mussolini	10
Common Man	17	Tyranny	7
Common Good	12	Absolutism	—
Free Enterprise	6	Anarchy	—
Consent of Governed	—*	Bolshevism	—
Reform	—	Despotism	—
Representative Gov't	—	Franco	—
Responsibility	—	Militarism	—
		Oppressive Laws	—
		Special Privilege	—
Total	2,974	Total	2,035

* Symbols when scored fewer than five times were not considered
to be statistically significant and were not included in final calcula-
tions.

TABLE XIX. NUMERICAL DISTRIBUTION OF POLITICAL
SYMBOLS CONSISTENT WITH THE AMERICAN CREED
BY SYMBOL AND CODE

Symbols	Total	(+1)	(−1)	(0)
Civil Liberties	592	508	19	65
Common Good	12	12	....	....
Common Man	17	11	....	6
Consent of Government	....*	....	....	....
Constitution U.S.	218	205	1	12
Democracy	286	262	6	18
Equality	465	446	10	9
F.E.P.C.	166	127	15	24
Freedom	201	193	2	6
Free Enterprise	6	4	1	1
Franchise	290	271	3	16
Independence	36	30	1	5
Justice	163	144	1	18
Liberty	58	58	....	....
Liberalism	143	124	6	13
Reform	....	....	....	....
Representative Government	....	....	....	....
Responsibility	....	....	....	....
Roosevelt	71	43	13	15
Supreme Court	250	181	10	59
Total	2,974	2,619	88	267
Percent	99.98	88.06	2.95	8.97

* Fewer than five symbols scored.

TABLE XX. NUMERICAL DISTRIBUTION OF POLITICAL
SYMBOLS OPPOSED TO AMERICAN CREED
BY SYMBOL AND CODE

Symbols	Total	(+1)	(−1)	(0)
Absolutism	....*	....	....	....
Anarchy	....	....	....	....
Bolshevism	....	....	....	....
Communism	183	10	101	72
Despotism	....	....	....	....
Dictatorship	27	....	25	2
Discrimination	561	12	541	8
Fascism	34	1	33	....
Franco	....	....	....	....
Hitler	56	....	51	5
Imperialism	44	5	34	5
Militarism	....	....	....	....
Mussolini	10	....	9	1
Nazism	32	....	31	1
Oppressive laws	....	....	....	....
Privilege Special	....	....	....	....
Poll Tax	110	4	86	20
Racism	257	7	242	8
Segregation	636	20	579	37
Slavery	51	....	46	5
Stalin	27	3	15	9
Tyranny	7	....	7	....
Total	2,035	62	1,800	173
Percent	99.99	3.04	88.45	8.50

* Fewer than five symbols scored.

BIBLIOGRAPHY

A. BOOKS

Aptheker, Herbert. *Negro Slave Revolts in the United States.* New York: International Publishers, 1939.

Ayer, N. W., and Son. *Directory of Newspapers and Periodicals.* Philadelphia, Pa.: 1949.

Beard, Charles A., and Mary. *The American Spirit.* New York: Macmillan Co., 1942.

Becker, Carl. *Freedom and Responsibility in the American Way of Life.* New York: Alfred A. Knopf, Inc., 1946.

Berry, Brewton. *Race Relations.* New York: Houghton Mifflin Company, 1951.

Bird, George, and Merwin, F.E. *The Newspaper and Society.* New York: Prentice-Hall, Inc., 1949.

Brogan, David W. *The American Character.* New York: Alfred A. Knopf, Inc., 1944.

Crowley, Herbert. *The Promise of American Life.* New York: Macmillan Co., 1909.

Curte, Merle. *The Growth of American Thought.* New York: Harper and Bros., 1943.

Davie, Maurice R. *Negroes in American Society.* New York: McGraw Hill Book Co., Inc., 1949.

Detweiler, F.G. *The Negro Press in the United States.* Chicago: University of Chicago Press, 1922.

de Tocqueville, Alexis. *Democracy in America.* Oxford University Press, Galaxy Edition, 1947.

Doob, Leonard. *Public Opinion and Propaganda.* New York: Henry Holt and Co., 1947.

Drake, St. C., and Cayton, H. *Black Metropolis.* New York: Harcourt Brace and Co., 1945.

Du Bois, W.E.B. *The Souls of Black Folk.* Chicago: A.C. McClurg and Co., 12th edition, 1920.

Edwards, Allen L. *Statistical Analysis.* New York: Rinehart and Co., Inc., 1946.

Franklin, John H. *From Slavery to Freedom.* New York: Alfred A. Knopf, 1950.

Frazier, E.F. *The Negro in the United States.* New York: Macmillan Co., 1949.

Hacker, Louis M. *The Shaping of the American Tradition.* New York: Columbia University Press, 1946.

Hughes, Helen M. *News and the Human Interest Story.* Chicago: University of Chicago Press, 1939.

Kerlin, Robert T. *The Voice of the Negro.* New York: E.P. Dutton and Co., 1919.

Kingsbury, Susan M. and Hart, H. *Newspapers and the News.* New York: G.P. Putnam's Sons Co., 1937.

Lundberg, George. *Social Research.* New York: Longman's Green and Co., 1942.

Lynd, R.S. *Knowledge For What.* Princeton: Princeton University Press, 1939.

Mott, Frank L. *American Journalism.* New York: Macmillan Co., 1950.

Murray, Florence. (Editor). *The Negro Handbook.* New York: Macmillan Co., 1949.

Myrdal, Gunnar. *An American Dilemma.* New York: Harper and Bros., 1944.

Monroe, Work. (Editor). *Negro Year Book.* Tuskegee Institute, 1921-22.

Norton, T.G. *The Constitution of the United States.* New York: America's Future Inc., 1946.

Oak, V.V. *The Negro Newspaper.* Yellow Springs, Ohio: Antioch College Press, 1948.

Parrington, Vernon L. *Main Springs in American Thought.* New York: Harcourt Brace and Co., 1930.

Penn, I. Garland. *The Afro-American Press and Its Editors.* Springfield, Mass.: Willey and Co., 1891.

Rourke, Constance. *The Roots of American Culture.* New York: Harcourt Brace and Co., 1942.

Smith, Bernard. (Editor). *The Democratic Spirit.* New York: Alfred A. Knopf, Inc., 1945.

Smith, B.L., Laswell, H.D., and Casey, R.D. *Propaganda Communication and Public Opinion.* Princeton: Princeton University Press.

Tyler, Alice F. (Editor). *Freedom's Ferment.* Minneapolis: University of Minnesota Press, 1944.

Willey, M.M. *The Country Newspaper.* Chapel Hill: University of North Carolina Press, 1926.

Woodward, J.L. *Foreign News in American Newspapers.* New York: Columbia University Press, 1930.

B. ARTICLES, BULLETINS, MONOGRAPHS, ETC.

Brown, Warren H. "A Negro Looks at the Negro Press." *Saturday Review of Literature*. XXV, No. 51, (December 19, 1947), pp. 5, 6.

Bureau of the Census. Negro Newspapers and Periodicals in the United States. Washington, D.C.: Government Printing Office, Bulletin No. 1, (1945).

Burma, John H. "An Analysis of the Present Negro Press," *Social Forces*, XXVI, No. 2, (December, 1947), pp. 172-180.

Chambliss, Rollin. *What Negro Newspapers in Georgia Are Saying About Some Social Problems*. Unpublished Master's thesis, University of Georgia: 1934.

Dabney, Virginius. "Nearer and Nearer the Precipice." *Atlantic Monthly*, 171, No. 1, (January, 1943), pp. 94-101.

Davidson, Philip. "An Analysis of the Soviet Controlled Berlin Press." *Public Opinion Quarterly*, VII, No. 1, (March, 1947), pp. 40-57.

Detweiler, F.G. "The Negro Press Today." *American Journal of Sociology*, XLIV, No. 3, (November, 1938), pp. 391-401.

"Fortune Press Analysis: Negro Press." *Fortune*, XXXI, No. 5, (May, 1945).

Gordon, Eugene. "Outstanding Negro Newspapers." *Opportunity*, V, (December, 1927), pp. 358-363.

Gordon, Eugene. "The Negro Press." *Annals* of the American Academy of Political and Social Science, CXXXX, No. 6 (November, 1928), pp. 248-256.

Hershaw, L.M. "Negro Press in America." *Charities and Commons*, XV, No. 10, (October, 1905), pp. 66-68.

Johnson, Charles S. "The Rise of the Negro Magazine." *Journal of Negro History*, XIII, No. 1, (January, 1928), pp. 7-21.

Jones, Dewey R. *Effect of the Negro Press on Race Relationship in the South*. Unpublished Master's thesis, Columbia University, 1932.

Laswell, Harold D. "The Politically Significant Content of the Press: Coding Procedures." *Journalism Quarterly*, XIX, No. 1, (March, 1942), pp. 12-24.

Laswell, Harold D. "The World Attention Survey." *Public Opinion Quarterly*, V. No. 4, (December, 1941), pp. 456-62.

Lee, Wallace. "Does the Negro Press Speak for Most Negroes in Its Opinions " *Negro Digest*, I, No. 4, (February, 1943), p. 54.

Oak, V.V. "What About the Negro Press?" *Saturday Review of Literature*, XXVI, No. 10, (March 6, 1943), pp. 4, 5.

Prattis, P.L. "Racial Segregation and Negro Journalism." *Phylon*, VIII, No. 4, (December, 1947), pp. 305-314.

Sancton, Thomas. "The Negro Press." *New Republic*, 108, No. 17, (April 26, 1943), pp. 557-561.